AF424610

SEOULMATES IN THE MAKING

KANIESHA JOSHI.

Copyright © Kaniesha Joshi.
All Rights Reserved.

This book has been self-published with all reasonable efforts taken to make the material error-free by the author. No part of this book shall be used, reproduced in any manner whatsoever without written permission from the author, except in the case of brief quotations embodied in critical articles and reviews.

The Author of this book is solely responsible and liable for its content including but not limited to the views, representations, descriptions, statements, information, opinions and references ["Content"]. The Content of this book shall not constitute or be construed or deemed to reflect the opinion or expression of the Publisher or Editor. Neither the Publisher nor Editor endorse or approve the Content of this book or guarantee the reliability, accuracy or completeness of the Content published herein and do not make any representations or warranties of any kind, express or implied, including but not limited to the implied warranties of merchantability, fitness for a particular purpose. The Publisher and Editor shall not be liable whatsoever for any errors, omissions, whether such errors or omissions result from negligence, accident, or any other cause or claims for loss or damages of any kind, including without limitation, indirect or consequential loss or damage arising out of use, inability to use, or about the reliability, accuracy or sufficiency of the information contained in this book.

Made with ♥ on the Notion Press Platform
www.notionpress.com

Kang Ji-ae's time at Yongpa High in Busan was a difficult chapter in her life. She was often bullied for her appearance, with classmates making cruel remarks about her being "fat." The constant teasing and exclusion made her feel isolated and self-conscious, and she struggled with her self-esteem during those years. Despite the harsh treatment, Ji-ae kept to herself, focusing on her studies and dreaming of a better future. The experience shaped her resilience and determination, helping her grow stronger and more confident as she moved forward in life.

So, read on to indulge in Ji-ae's new experience at her new school in Seoul.

It was Ji-ae's first day at Titan Academy. She had transferred from her old school, Yongpa High in Busan. She was on her way to Titan Academy, signing up and heading to her assigned dorm. As she opened the door she saw three of her other roommates, chatting and having a cup of coffee.

"Oh! You must be our fourth roommate! Welcome to Titan Academy!" said Su-ah, with a smile on her face.

"Thanks! I'm Kang Ji-ae. And you?"

"I'm Kang Su-jin."

"I'm Madeline."

"And I'm Su-ah. Pleasure to meet you!"

"You too!"

They had a nice chat before getting ready for school.

"So, tell me more about yourself." said Su-ah.

"I moved here from my old school in Busan. My mom is Korean and my dad is Indian." replied Ji-ae.

"Wow, Ji-ae! You have such amazing parents!" exclaimed Su-jin.

"They'll be so happy to hear that! <3" said Ji-ae.

Once they finished getting ready, they left their dorm and sat together during assembly. That was when Ji-ae saw Soo-ho.

"Ooh who's that?" asked Ji-ae.

"That's Soo-ho. He's one of my good friends. He's kind of cold, but I could introduce you if you want." replied Su-jin.

"That would be nice!" said Ji-ae, with excitement.

After a while, Ji-ae asked,

"Who is that?"

"Oh. That's Lim Ju-kyung. She just broke up with Soo-ho a few months ago." replied Su-ah.

"Oh..." said Ji-ae

After assembly, Ji-ae's first class was Literature.

"Annyeonghaseyo. I am Han Jun-woo and I will be your new literature teacher. Before we start, I would like to assign you your partners."

Coincidentally, Ji-ae and Soo-ho got paired together.

"Hello. I'm Ji-ae. And you?"

No response

"Su-jin told me about you." said Ji-ae, trying to break the silence.

Still no response

Then there was a pause for a few seconds, meanwhile, Ji-ae already knew she had a crush on him. Then Soo-ho suddenly asked

"So, do you know how to speak Korean?"

"물론 저는 한국어를 알아요! 다른 사람들과 어떻게 소통하겠어요?

(Of course I know Korean! How else would I communicate with other people?)"

"Good. I've never seen a foreigner speak in Korean before." said Soo-ho.

Ji-ae was offended. She thought to herself

Wow...rude much?

But deep down, she knew...she had a thing for him.

After the school day ended, all the girls met up in their dorm.

"Who's up for a 'first day of school' slumber party?!" asked Su-ah, with a lot of excitement.

"Meeeeeee!!" replied Ji-ae.

"Me too!!" exclaimed Madeline.

"Do we really have to do this on the first day?" asked Su-jin.

"Yup!" replied Su-ah.

At their slumber party in their dorm, they played many fun games. They had pillow fights, played never have I ever, charades, would you rather, made the most crazy outfits with any clothes they could find and had the best day ever! Then, they started playing truth or dare. Su-ah asked the next question.

"Okay, Ji-ae, Truth or Dare?"

"Hmm...Truth!" replied Ji-ae.

"Okay. Do you have a crush on somebody?" asked Su-ah.

"......Yes." answered Ji-ae.

"Oooohhh who is it? Is it Soo-ho?" asked Su-jin.

"Hey! Only one question per round!" said Ji-ae.

"Okay okay....Wait you're not denying it!" said Madeline.

"Can we please just change the topic?" requested Ji-ae.

"Okay fine but just remember that I'm gonna ask you that same question next round." said Su-jin.

Ji-ae rolled her eyes but couldn't stop her laughter. They all laughed. Little did they know, they were definitely not prepared for the next day...

"Okay...Soo-ah! Truth or Dare?" asked Madeline.

"Dare!" exclaimed Su-ah.

"Hmm...ooh! I got one! Call someone and pretend it's their birthday." said Ji-ae.

"Oooohh...who should I call??"

"I know! Yoo Tae-hoon (Su-ah's boyfriend)!" said Su-jin.

"Hmm okay."

After they finished playing, they went to bed.

"Goodnight, my chingu-deul (plural, friends)!" exclaimed Su-ah.

"Goodnight!" replied Ji-ae.

Ji-ae's first day at Titan Academy was amazing! But the highlight of her day was making new friends, unlike at her old school, Yongpa High in Busan.

The next morning, Ji-ae woke up to the sound of her alarm blaring at full volume. She groaned, turning over to check the time.

7:30 AM.

"Oh no! We're gonna be late!" Ji-ae panicked, throwing off her blanket.

Su-ah, Su-jin, and Madeline all groaned in unison.

"Just five more minutes..." Su-ah mumbled, burying her face in her pillow.

"Nope! Get up! We need to hurry!" Ji-ae said, pulling Su-ah's blanket away.

Madeline rubbed her eyes and yawned. "Ugh... why did we sleep so late?"

"Because someone—*cough* Su-ah—*cough* dared us to do ridiculous things all night," Su-jin said, sitting up with messy hair.

"Hey! I was just making memories," Su-ah defended with a pout.

After a rushed morning routine, they sprinted to class, barely making it in time before the bell rang. Ji-ae sighed in relief as she plopped down into her seat. But her relief was short-lived when she noticed the person sitting next to her.

It was Soo-ho.

He glanced at her briefly but said nothing. Ji-ae nervously tucked a strand of hair behind her ear, her heart racing. *Why am I so nervous?*

Han Jun-woo entered the classroom, carrying a stack of books. "Alright, class. Today, we're starting a group project on classic literature. You'll be working in pairs."

Ji-ae's stomach dropped. She had almost forgotten about the literature partner assignment.

"You and I need to meet after school to work on the project," Soo-ho said suddenly, his deep voice breaking the silence.

Ji-ae blinked. *Did he actually just talk to me first?*

"Uh… yeah, sure! Where do you wanna meet?"

"The library. Don't be late."

Before Ji-ae could say anything else, Soo-ho turned his attention back to the lesson.

After school, Ji-ae made her way to the library, her heart thumping in anticipation. When she arrived, Soo-ho was already there, flipping through a book absentmindedly.

"You're on time," he noted without looking up.

"Well, I didn't want to get scolded by my **oh-so-serious** partner," Ji-ae teased, taking a seat.

Soo-ho's lips twitched slightly, but he didn't respond. Ji-ae decided to focus on the project, but as they worked, she couldn't help but steal glances at him.

Why do I feel like there's more to him than just his cold personality?

Just then, a familiar voice interrupted her thoughts.

"Oh, Soo-ho! What a coincidence."

Ji-ae looked up to see Lim Ju-kyung standing there, a cunning smile on her face and her arms crossed as she stared at Soo-ho.

Soo-ho's expression darkened. "What do you want?"

"I didn't expect to see you here... with her," Ju-kyung said, glancing at Ji-ae with a fake smile.

Ji-ae felt a strange tension in the air. Was there still something between them?

And why did she suddenly feel... jealous?

Ji-ae shifted uncomfortably in her seat as Lim Ju-kyung continued to stare at her. There was something about her presence that made Ji-ae feel like she didn't belong.

Soo-ho, on the other hand, looked completely indifferent. He flipped another page in his book and didn't even glance up.

"Do you need something?" he asked, his voice as cold as ever.

Ju-kyung pouted. "I was just surprised, that's all. It's rare to see you working with someone new. Especially someone like... her."

Ji-ae's heart dropped. *Someone like me?*

Soo-ho finally looked up, his brows furrowed. "What's that supposed to mean?"

"Oh, nothing," Ju-kyung said sweetly, her eyes never leaving Ji-ae. "I just think it's cute, that's all."

Ji-ae felt her hands clench into fists under the table. She had heard that tone before—the same tone the girls at her old school used right before they tore her apart with their words.

She could already feel the whispers and stares from the other students in the library.

Before she could say anything, Soo-ho closed his book and stood up. "We're busy. And if you're not here to help, then leave."

Ju-kyung pouted but finally walked away, her heels clicking against the tiled floor.

Ji-ae sighed and shook her head. "What was **that** about?"

Soo-ho shrugged, leaning back in his chair. "She likes to act like she still has a say in my life."

"So... you guys broke up for a reason?" Ji-ae asked, her curiosity getting the best of her.

Soo-ho's gaze darkened. "It doesn't matter."

Ji-ae frowned. "But—"

"I don't talk about it," he cut her off sharply.

That was enough of a warning for Ji-ae to drop it.

They continued working in awkward silence for a while, but Ji-ae's mind was swirling with thoughts. *Is he really over her? What if he still likes her? Why does this bother me so much?*

Just then, Soo-ho broke the silence. "Why did you transfer to Titan Academy?"

Ji-ae hesitated. *Should I tell him?* She didn't want his pity. She didn't want him to look at her the way people at her old school did.

"It's... complicated," she finally said, avoiding his gaze.

Soo-ho didn't push. He simply nodded. "I see."

Ji-ae was surprised by his reaction. No mocking, no prying. Just a simple acceptance of her answer. She felt a strange warmth in her chest.

Suddenly, Madeline came running into the library, nearly knocking over a chair. "Ji-ae! Emergency! Su-ah needs us!"

Ji-ae immediately stood up. "What happened?"

"She got caught trying to sneak food into class, and now she has to clean the entire cafeteria after school!" Madeline groaned.

Ji-ae turned to Soo-ho. "Um... can we work on this tomorrow? I don't want to leave Su-ah alone."

For a moment, Soo-ho didn't respond. His cold, unreadable expression made Ji-ae nervous. But then, to her surprise, he sighed and stood up.

"I'll help," he said, grabbing his books.

Ji-ae's eyes widened. "Wait, what?"

"You said you don't want to leave her alone. I'll help too," he said casually. "Let's go."

Ji-ae didn't have time to process what had just happened. She simply followed after him, her heart doing somersaults in her chest.

Was Soo-ho... being nice to her?

And why did that make her heart race even more? Ji-ae was confused.

As they walked into the cafeteria, Su-jin asked Ji-ae, her voice barely above a whisper.

"Hey, by the way, how is Soo-ho sweet to you? Did you say anything?"

"Uhm...I-I don't know actually." replied Ji-ae, half of her mind still confused."

Just then, Su-ah saw them.

"OH MY GOD MY CHINGU-DEUL! WHERE WERE YOU GUYS?"

"I was working on my project at the library with Soo-ho. But don't worry! We're here to help you clean the cafeteria" replied Ji-ae.

"Yea! Let's get cleaning!" said Su-jin and Madeline.

"I'll help too." said Soo-ho.

Su-ah's eyes widened in shock as she stared at Soo-ho. "Wait, what? You're helping too?"

Soo-ho simply shrugged. "It'll be faster if more people help."

Ji-ae couldn't believe what she was hearing. Just earlier, Soo-ho had been his usual cold and distant self, and now he was volunteering to help? Was this some kind of alternate reality?

Su-jin smirked and elbowed Ji-ae playfully. "Aww, Soo-ho's being all nice. Ji-ae, are you sure you didn't bribe him or something?"

Ji-ae rolled her eyes. "Oh, shut up and start cleaning."

With that, they all grabbed some cleaning supplies and got to work. Su-ah was still pouting about being punished, but at least she had her friends with her. Madeline put on some music from her phone to make things more fun, and soon, they were all singing along as they wiped tables, swept the floor, and took out the trash.

At one point, Ji-ae was struggling to reach a high shelf to wipe it down. She stood on her tiptoes, stretching her arm as far as it would go, but she still couldn't quite reach.

Suddenly, a hand reached over hers and effortlessly wiped the spot clean. She turned to see Soo-ho standing next to her, casually finishing the job without a word.

Her heart skipped a beat.

"Uh... thanks," Ji-ae muttered, looking away quickly to hide her flustered face.

"Be more careful next time," Soo-ho said simply before moving on.

Su-ah, who had witnessed the moment, gasped dramatically. "OMG, Ji-ae, are you blushing?"

Ji-ae shot her a warning glare. "I am NOT."

"Mmm-hmm," Su-ah hummed teasingly, but before she could say anything more, Madeline grabbed her and spun her around in a playful dance. "Less teasing, more cleaning!"

After what felt like hours, they finally finished cleaning. Su-ah wiped the sweat off her forehead and collapsed onto a nearby chair. "I'm never sneaking food into class again."

Su-jin snorted. "Yeah, right. You'll probably do it again next week."

Su-ah grinned sheepishly. "Maybe."

Ji-ae sighed and took a seat as well, exhausted but oddly happy. It was strange—back at her old school, she would have never imagined herself surrounded by such great friends. And as for Soo-ho... well, he was still a mystery, but maybe, just maybe, he wasn't as cold as he pretended to be.

As they were packing up to leave, Soo-ho turned to Ji-ae. "Don't forget. We still have to finish the project. Library. Tomorrow."

Ji-ae nodded. "Got it."

With that, Soo-ho walked off, leaving Ji-ae staring after him. Su-jin nudged her. "Admit it, you're starting to like him more."

Ji-ae groaned. "Can we not start this again?"

Su-ah giggled. "Ooooh, you totally are!"

Madeline clapped her hands together. "Okay, enough teasing. Who wants bubble tea? My treat!"

"Me!" Su-ah and Su-jin shouted in unison, practically dragging Ji-ae along before she could protest.

As they left the classroom, Ji-ae stole one last glance down the hallway where Soo-ho had disappeared. She shook her head, pushing away the thoughts swirling in her mind.

Maybe Su-jin and Su-ah were being ridiculous.

Maybe.

But deep down, she wasn't so sure anymore.

The next day, Ji-ae walked into the library, expecting another quiet and awkward study session with Soo-ho. Instead, she was greeted by a familiar voice.

"Ji-ae! There you are. I was looking for you."

She turned around and blinked in surprise. "Han Seo-jun? What are you doing here?"

He grinned, running a hand through his messy brown hair. "I figured I'd help you with the project. Soo-ho doesn't own the tutoring rights, does he?"

Ji-ae chuckled. "I don't think so, but he might act like he does."

"Tch," Seo-jun smirked. "Sounds like him. Anyway, let's get to work."

They sat down together, flipping through books and discussing their project. To Ji-ae's surprise, Seo-jun was not only helpful but also easy to talk to. He cracked jokes, teased her lightly, and even helped her with a particularly confusing part of their research.

Meanwhile, Soo-ho arrived a few minutes later, his eyes narrowing slightly when he saw them sitting together, laughing at something Seo-jun had said. He clenched his jaw and dropped his bag onto the table with a loud thud.

Ji-ae glanced up. "Oh, hey, Soo-ho! Seo-jun's helping us out too."

Soo-ho slid into the seat next to Ji-ae, his expression unreadable. "Great. The more, the merrier."

But his tone was flat, and Ji-ae couldn't help but notice the way his fingers tapped against the table impatiently. Seo-jun, of course, seemed oblivious—or maybe he was just enjoying Soo-ho's annoyance.

"So, Ji-ae," Seo-jun continued, leaning a little closer, "what do you think? Should we add this part to the presentation, or does it make things too complicated?"

Ji-ae hummed, considering it. "I think it works, but maybe we should simplify it a little.

Seo-jun smiled. "Smart and pretty. Nice."

Ji-ae's breath hitched as she met his gaze. The warmth in his eyes made her pulse race, her fingers curling against the table.

Soo-ho's chair scraped against the floor as he shifted. "Let's finish this first."
Ji-ae raised an eyebrow at his sudden irritation, but before she could say anything, Seo-jun leaned in and whispered, "Is he always this grumpy?"

Ji-ae snorted, biting back a laugh. "Pretty much."

Soo-ho shot them a look. "I can hear you, you know."

Seo-jun smirked. "Good."

As they continued working, Ji-ae found herself getting more comfortable around Seo-jun. He was warm, funny, and easy to be around. But every time she laughed at one of his jokes or leaned in to discuss something, she could feel Soo-ho's gaze burning into them.

Then, out of nowhere, Soo-ho slammed his book shut, making Ji-ae and Seo-jun jump.

"I'm done here," he muttered, standing up abruptly.

Ji-ae frowned. "Wait, we're not finished—"

"You two seem to be doing just fine without me," Soo-ho snapped, grabbing his bag and walking out of the library before Ji-ae could respond.

Seo-jun raised an eyebrow. "Yikes. Someone's in a mood."

Ji-ae sighed, watching Soo-ho disappear through the doors. She had never seen him like that before..."He's always like that."

Seo-jun nudged her playfully. ""Come on, let's take a break." Seo-jun suggested, nudging her toward the door. "You look like you need some fresh air."

They stepped outside, the cool breeze brushing against Ji-ae's skin. The air between them grew heavy, charged with something neither of them wanted to name. Ji-ae's heart pounded against her ribs as she stared into Seo-jun's deep, intense eyes. The warmth of his hand on hers sent shivers down her spine, making it impossible to ignore the way he was looking at her.

"You know," Seo-jun murmured, his voice lower than usual, almost teasing, "for someone who claims to hate me, you sure seem comfortable right now."

Ji-ae scoffed, rolling her eyes even as she felt her face heat up. "Don't flatter yourself. I just... don't find you as annoying as before."

He smirked, leaning in slightly, making the distance between them disappear little by little. "That's progress, I guess."

Ji-ae wanted to say something, anything to break the thick tension between them, but words failed her. She could smell the faint scent of his cologne, mixed with the freshness of the night air. Her pulse quickened when she realized just how close they were.

Seo-jun must have noticed because his smirk softened into something more genuine. "You've got something on your face."

Ji-ae blinked. "Huh?"

He reached out, brushing his thumb just under her lip, his touch featherlight. She froze, breath hitching in her throat. Was this real? Was Han Seo-jun actually doing this?

Her lips parted slightly, and for a moment, she thought he was going to pull away, but instead, he stayed, his thumb lingering against her skin longer than necessary. The way his eyes darkened made her stomach do somersaults.

"There," he murmured, voice husky. "Got it."

Ji-ae swallowed hard, trying to regain control of herself, but then Seo-jun did something completely unexpected—he tucked a strand of her hair behind her ear, his fingers barely grazing her skin. The touch sent another wave of warmth through her, making her toes curl inside her shoes.

"You should be more careful," he said, his voice almost a whisper now. "I might start thinking you actually like me."

Ji-ae let out a shaky breath, gathering the last of her composure. "And what if I do?" she asked, barely above a whisper, surprising even herself with her own words.

Seo-jun's eyes flashed with something unreadable—surprise, amusement, and something deeper. Then, before she could think twice about what she just said, he tilted his head slightly, gaze dropping to her lips. Her breath hitched, anticipation thick in the air between them.

And then it happened.

Seo-jun leaned in slowly, giving her every chance to move away. But she didn't. Instead, she found herself closing the remaining distance between them, her lips brushing against his in the softest, most hesitant touch at first. But then, the hesitation melted away, replaced by something warmer, something deeper.

His hand moved to her waist, pulling her just a little closer, while her fingers curled into the fabric of his jacket. The kiss was slow at first, almost unsure, but then Seo-jun angled his head, deepening it, his hand tightening slightly on her waist as if he never wanted to let go.

Ji-ae felt like she was floating, completely lost in the sensation of his lips against hers. Everything else faded away—the cool night air, the faint sounds of the city in the distance—until it was just them.

When they finally broke apart, both slightly breathless, Seo-jun let out a low chuckle, his forehead resting against hers. "That didn't feel like hate to me."

Ji-ae bit her lip, feeling her cheeks heat up. "Shut up," she muttered, lightly smacking his arm, but even she couldn't hide the small smile tugging at her lips.

Seo-jun grinned, brushing his fingers lightly against her cheek. "I knew you couldn't resist me."

Ji-ae groaned, pushing him away playfully, but the truth was, her heart was still racing.

What did this mean for them now? And more importantly, what would Soo-ho think if he found out?

Soo-ho stood frozen, his fists clenched at his sides. He had seen everything—the way Ji-ae looked at Seo-jun, the way she let him touch her, the way she kissed him back. His mind screamed at him to move, to say something, but he couldn't. He felt like the air had been knocked out of his lungs.

Ji-ae turned, her eyes widening in shock when she saw him. "Soo-ho..."

His jaw tightened, his expression unreadable. "I didn't expect this." His voice was dangerously calm, but Ji-ae could hear the tension laced within it.

"I—" she started, but no words came out. What could she even say? That it was a mistake? That it didn't mean anything? Because that would be a lie.

Seo-jun stepped forward, his usual smirk gone. "Soo-ho, it's not what you think."

Soo-ho let out a bitter laugh. "Not what I think? Then tell me, Seo-jun, what exactly am I supposed to think when I see this?"

Ji-ae's stomach twisted painfully. "Soo-ho, please, let me explain."

But he shook his head, taking a step back. "I don't think I want to hear it." His eyes, filled with something between hurt and disbelief, flickered between her and Seo-jun before he turned away, walking off into the night without another word.

Ji-ae felt her chest tighten, panic rising within her. "Soo-ho!" she called after him, but he didn't stop. He didn't even look back.

She could feel Seo-jun watching her, but she couldn't focus on him right now. All she could think about was the pain in Soo-ho's eyes before he walked away—the look of someone who had just lost something important, even if he didn't know exactly what it was.

Ji-ae stood frozen, her breath shaky as she watched Soo-ho disappear into the night. A cold, sinking feeling settled in her chest, and she clenched her hands into fists, trying to push away the guilt clawing at her.

"Ji-ae," Seo-jun's voice was softer now, lacking its usual teasing edge. "Are you okay?"

She turned to him, eyes wide with uncertainty. "I don't know."

Seo-jun sighed, rubbing the back of his neck. "Look, I didn't mean to make things complicated for you."

Ji-ae shook her head. "It's not just you. It's... everything." Her voice wavered. "Soo-ho—he looked..."

"Hurt?" Seo-jun finished for her, his gaze flickering with something unreadable. "Do you—do you like him?"

Ji-ae opened her mouth but hesitated. Did she? Her heart ached seeing Soo-ho like that, but it wasn't just guilt—there was something deeper, something she hadn't allowed herself to acknowledge until now.

Seo-jun sighed again. "You don't have to answer that." His voice was strangely quiet, almost resigned. "But whatever this is, you need to figure it out. Because if you don't, someone's going to end up getting hurt."

Ji-ae nodded slowly, the weight of his words pressing down on her. She needed to talk to Soo-ho. She needed to make things right. But the question was—how?

Ji-ae couldn't sleep that night. Every time she closed her eyes, she saw Soo-ho's expression—his clenched jaw, his fists at his sides, and worst of all, the look in his eyes before he turned away.

By morning, she knew she had to talk to him.

She found him in the hallway at school, standing by his locker. He looked up when he saw her, his face unreadable.

"Soo-ho, can we talk?" Ji-ae asked hesitantly.

He exhaled through his nose but nodded, shutting his locker. "Yeah, sure."

They walked to a quieter corner of the school. Ji-ae wrung her hands together, trying to find the right words. "About last night... I—"

"You don't have to explain." Soo-ho cut her off, his tone unnervingly calm. "You like Seo-jun, right?"

Ji-ae blinked, thrown off. "I—um..."

Soo-ho gave a small, forced smile. "It's okay. You don't have to feel bad about it. If you're happy with him, I'm fine with it."

Her heart twisted at his words. "Soo-ho, are you sure?"

"Yeah," he said quickly. Too quickly. "I mean, it's not like I had any claim on you or anything."

Ji-ae studied him, searching for a sign that he was lying, but his mask was firmly in place. Finally, she let out a slow breath. "Okay."

That afternoon, she found Seo-jun leaning against a classroom door, talking to a few other students. When he spotted her, he grinned. "Well, well, if it isn't my favorite person."

Ji-ae rolled her eyes but couldn't fight the small smile forming on her lips. "Seo-jun..."

"Yeah?" He smirked.

She took a deep breath, then reached for his hand. "Let's do this. Let's give it a real shot."

For the first time, Seo-jun looked genuinely surprised. His teasing demeanor faltered for just a second before he laced his fingers with hers, his grip warm and firm. "You sure?"

Ji-ae nodded. "I am."

A slow grin spread across his face. "Well then, who am I to say no?"

And just like that, the news spread like wildfire. By lunchtime, everyone at Titan Academy knew that Ji-ae and Seo-jun were together. They walked through the cafeteria hand in hand, drawing stares and whispers from their classmates.

Denise raised an eyebrow as she sat down at their table. "So, this is real, huh?"

"Very real," Seo-jun said smugly, throwing an arm around Ji-ae's shoulders.

Ji-ae elbowed him, but her cheeks were already burning.

Across the cafeteria, Soo-ho sat with his usual group, laughing at something JianHao said. But every now and then, his gaze flickered toward Ji-ae and Seo-jun.

And each time, his smile faded just a little.

For the next few days, Ji-ae and Seo-jun were the center of attention at Titan Academy. Everywhere they went, people whispered, stared, and even giggled. It was like they had become the main characters in a school drama, and honestly, Ji-ae wasn't sure how she felt about it.

"Why is everyone acting like we're celebrities?" she muttered as they walked down the hallway.

Seo-jun smirked, swinging their hands slightly. "Maybe because we're the hottest couple in school now?"

Ji-ae shot him a glare, but he just grinned wider. "Relax, princess. Let them talk."

She sighed, trying to ignore the way her heart still did a weird flip every time he called her that.

At lunch, she slid into her usual seat next to Denise, while Seo-jun plopped down beside her, draping his arm lazily over the back of her chair. JianHao raised an eyebrow at them.

"Okay, I have to ask," he said, leaning forward. "How did this even happen? Weren't you guys always at each other's throats?"

Seo-jun smirked. "Some would call that romantic tension."

Ji-ae groaned, covering her face with her hands. "Don't listen to him."

Denise snorted. "Honestly, I never thought I'd see the day. But you two are kinda... cute?"

Debbie smirked. "I give it a month."

Seo-jun gasped dramatically. "Wow. No faith in us at all?"

Before Debbie could reply, Ji-ae felt it—the shift in the air. A presence behind her. She turned slightly and locked eyes with Soo-ho, who had just walked past their table.

For a moment, it was like time froze.

His face was unreadable, but something flickered in his eyes. Something that made her stomach twist uncomfortably. Then, just like that, he turned away, joining his own table as if nothing had happened.

Ji-ae swallowed hard.

Seo-jun, who had been watching the interaction, suddenly tightened his grip on her hand. He didn't say anything, but she could feel it—he wasn't as unaffected by Soo-ho's presence as he pretended to be.

"Ji-ae," he murmured, just low enough for her to hear.

She turned back to him, and his expression was serious for once.

"You're mine now, right?"

She hesitated for only a second before nodding. "Yeah."

That was all Seo-jun needed. His smirk returned, and without warning, he leaned in, brushing a kiss against her temple right in front of everyone.

The entire cafeteria erupted into gasps and whispers.

Ji-ae's face burned as she smacked his arm. "Yah!"

Seo-jun just laughed. "What? Just proving a point."

But across the cafeteria, Soo-ho sat rigid in his seat, his fingers clenched tightly around his chopsticks.

JianHao, who had been watching him carefully, nudged his arm. "You okay, bro?"

Soo-ho forced a chuckle. "Of course. Why wouldn't I be?"

But as he glanced back at Ji-ae and Seo-jun, laughing and teasing each other, he felt something twist painfully in his chest.

Because no matter how much he lied to himself...

He was definitely not okay.

The days passed, and Ji-ae and Seo-jun became inseparable. They walked to class together, teased each other nonstop, and even shared snacks during breaks. To everyone at Titan Academy, they were the ultimate couple—effortlessly cool and impossible to ignore.

But no matter how much she tried to focus on Seo-jun, Ji-ae couldn't shake the feeling that something was off. Or rather, someone.

Soo-ho.

Every time she glanced at him, he was already looking away. Whenever their paths crossed, he acted normal—too normal. He would flash that easy smile of his, joke around with his friends, and pretend like nothing had changed.

But Ji-ae knew better.

It was in the small things—the way his laughter didn't quite reach his eyes, the way he avoided standing too close to her, the way his hands clenched into fists whenever Seo-jun casually slung an arm around her shoulders.

It was all an act.

And it was driving her crazy.

Finally, one afternoon, she had enough.

After school, she found him on the rooftop, leaning against the railing with his back to her.

"You're a terrible liar, you know that?"

Soo-ho stiffened for just a second before turning around, a smirk already in place. "Ji-ae. To what do I owe the honor?"

She crossed her arms, narrowing her eyes. "Cut the act, Soo-ho. I know you're not okay."

He let out a soft chuckle, shaking his head. "You're imagining things."

Ji-ae stepped closer, her gaze searching his face. "If you're really fine with this, then look me in the eyes and tell me you don't care."

For a split second, she saw it—the raw emotion flickering behind his gaze, the storm he was trying so hard to hide.

But then, just as quickly, he masked it again.

He shrugged. "I don't care."

Ji-ae's breath hitched.

"You and Seo-jun are together now. I'm happy for you."

Liar.

She knew it. He knew it. But he still said it.

Ji-ae's heart clenched painfully, but what could she do? He was giving her an answer. He was telling her to move on.

So she nodded. "Okay."

Soo-ho smiled, but it didn't reach his eyes. "See? No big deal."

Ji-ae wanted to scream at him, to shake him until he admitted the truth. But instead, she forced a smile of her own. "Yeah. No big deal."

And just like that, they both became liars.

The next day, she walked into school hand-in-hand with Seo-jun, forcing herself not to look back.

But Soo-ho was watching.

And for the first time, he realized—losing Ji-ae wasn't just painful.

It was unbearable.

Titan Academy was buzzing.

Ji-ae and Seo-jun had officially become *that* couple—the one everyone talked about, the one that turned heads whenever they walked into a room.

Girls whispered about how lucky Ji-ae was.

Guys muttered about how Seo-jun really won this time.

And Soo-ho?

He just smiled and acted like nothing was wrong.

But inside?

He was *losing his mind.*

Every time he saw Seo-jun drape his arm around Ji-ae, every time he heard her laugh at one of his dumb jokes, every time she looked at Seo-jun the way she *used* to look at him…

It felt like someone was ripping his heart out and setting it on fire.

Yet, he still said nothing.

Not until that day.

The day everything *snapped.*

It happened in the cafeteria.

Ji-ae and Seo-jun were sitting with their usual group, and for once, Soo-ho had joined them, keeping up his whole *I'm totally fine, nothing bothers me* act.

Ji-ae tried not to focus on him, but it was *impossible.*

He was laughing. He was joking around. He was being *so normal* that it pissed her off.

"Hey, babe, try this," Seo-jun said, holding out a spoonful of food toward her.

Ji-ae blushed slightly but leaned in to take a bite.

And that was the moment.

The moment Soo-ho's grip on his chopsticks *snapped.*

Literally.

A loud *crack* echoed through the cafeteria as the chopsticks in his hand broke clean in half.

Silence.

Everyone turned to look at him.

Ji-ae's heart stopped.

Soo-ho blinked down at the broken pieces in his hands, his face unreadable.

"Wow, dude," Seo-jun laughed, clearly amused. "That's some serious strength. You mad about something?"

Ji-ae stiffened.

For a second, she thought Soo-ho was going to brush it off like he always did.

But instead, he looked straight at her.

His eyes burned with something dangerous.

"Yeah," he said, voice low. "I think I am."

Ji-ae's breath hitched.

The tension was *thick* now. Everyone around them exchanged nervous glances, sensing the storm brewing.

Seo-jun raised a brow, tilting his head. "And what exactly is your problem?"

Soo-ho smirked, but there was *nothing* friendly about it.

"My problem?" He leaned forward slightly, his eyes never leaving Ji-ae's. "You really wanna know?"

Ji-ae swallowed hard.

Because for the first time since this whole mess started—

Soo-ho wasn't hiding anymore.

Titan Academy had never seen a fight like this.

What started as a quiet argument at lunch had exploded into a *full-blown war* between Seo-jun and Soo-ho.

And Ji-ae was *stuck in the middle.*

Again.

"Just admit it, Soo-ho," Seo-jun snapped, standing up so fast that his chair screeched against the floor. "You're *not* fine. You *hate* seeing me with Ji-ae, don't you?"

Soo-ho scoffed, crossing his arms. "Why would I care who Ji-ae dates? She can be with whoever she wants." His voice was dripping with mockery. "Even if it's *you.*"

Ji-ae stiffened.

She knew that tone.

That *fake* indifference, the one Soo-ho always used when he was hurt but refused to show it.

And it pissed Seo-jun off.

"Then why do you keep acting like this, huh?" Seo-jun shot back, stepping closer. "Why do you get all weird every time I touch her? Why do you keep staring at her like she's some prize you *lost?*"

Ji-ae's breath caught in her throat.

People were watching now.

The entire cafeteria had gone silent, students whispering, waiting for the explosion.

And it came.

Because Soo-ho finally lost it.

"You think I lost?" he laughed coldly, eyes sharp as knives. "Funny. Because from where I'm standing, it looks like *you're* the one trying so hard to prove you actually won."

Seo-jun's jaw clenched.

"Guys, *stop*—" Ji-ae started, but they weren't listening.

Soo-ho kept going. "*What's wrong, Seo-jun?* Is it not enough that you got the girl? Or do you need to rub it in my face every second of the day to feel like you actually matter to her?"

Ji-ae gasped. "*Soo-ho!*"

Seo-jun's expression darkened. "At least *I'm* not the one lying to myself."

"Yeah? Then why do you keep looking at her like you're waiting for her to pick *me* instead?" Soo-ho shot back, voice deadly quiet.

A stunned silence followed.

Ji-ae felt her heart *drop.*

Her hands trembled as she looked between them, her vision blurring.

What... is happening?

"Both of you..." Her voice wavered, but they still weren't looking at her.

They were too busy *destroying* each other.

"Maybe I *am* waiting," Soo-ho admitted with a bitter smile. "Because deep down, we *both* know how this ends, don't we?"

That was it.

That was the moment Ji-ae *broke.*

Her hands curled into fists as hot tears welled up in her eyes.

"SHUT UP!" she screamed.

Soo-ho and Seo-jun froze.

Ji-ae's chest rose and fell rapidly, her breath uneven. "You guys don't even care how I feel, do you?! You're just using me to fight each other!"

"Ji-ae—" Seo-jun reached for her, but she stepped back.

"I *hate this!*" Her voice cracked. "*I hate you both!*"

And then—

Before either of them could say another word—

She turned and *ran*.

Tears blurred her vision as she shoved past the crowd, ignoring the gasps and whispers.

She didn't know where she was going.

She just knew she needed to get *away*.

Away from them.

Away from this mess.

Away from the ache in her chest that wouldn't stop growing.

Ji-ae didn't stop running.

Her lungs burned. Her vision blurred. But she didn't stop.

The school courtyard disappeared behind her. The hallways became a blur of faces she didn't recognize.

All she could hear was the pounding of her own heart.

And then—

She found herself outside.

The cool breeze hit her tear-streaked face as she stumbled toward the back of the school. A place no one ever went. A place where she could finally break down *alone.*

Her legs gave out, and she collapsed onto the pavement, her sobs coming out in gasps.

Why?

Why did it hurt so much?

Why did she feel like she was *losing* both of them?

Why did she let herself believe, even for a second, that this wouldn't end in disaster?

She pulled her knees to her chest, squeezing her eyes shut.

And then—

Footsteps.

Heavy. Rushed.

Someone was coming.

She barely had time to react before a voice—ragged and desperate—called her name.

"Ji-ae!"

She looked up.

And there he was.

Her breath hitched.

She wiped her tears away quickly, but it was useless—Soo-ho had already seen them.

He stood a few feet away, chest rising and falling like he'd been running after her. His usual calm expression was gone, replaced by something raw, something aching.

For a long moment, neither of them spoke. The only sound was Ji-ae's uneven breathing and the distant chatter of students who had no idea what was happening here.

And then—

"Why did you run?" Soo-ho asked, his voice strained.

Ji-ae let out a bitter laugh, shaking her head. "What do you think?"

Soo-ho clenched his jaw. "Because of Seo-jun?"

She flinched.

But she didn't answer.

She couldn't answer.

Because it wasn't just about Seo-jun. It was about him. It was about the way Soo-ho looked at her, the way he spoke to her, the way he pretended he was fine but kept pulling her back into his orbit anyway.

And she was tired.

"Tch," Soo-ho scoffed, running a hand through his hair. "You're seriously crying over him?"

His words stung, but Ji-ae refused to let them break her. She lifted her chin, eyes glistening. "No. I'm crying because of you, Soo-ho."

That made him freeze.

His lips parted slightly, as if he was about to say something—but nothing came out.

Ji-ae sucked in a shaky breath. "You lied to me. You said you were okay with this. With me and Seo-jun. But you're not, are you?"

Soo-ho's hands curled into fists at his sides. His gaze dropped to the ground for a second before meeting hers again. "...What does it matter?" he muttered.

Ji-ae's heart twisted painfully. "It matters to me!"

Silence.

For a second, she swore she saw something crack in his expression. The mask slipping. The truth threatening to spill out—

But then, in the blink of an eye, it was gone.

He forced out a dry chuckle, his eyes darkening. "I don't get it, Ji-ae. You chose him. So why are you here, crying like this? Why do you care so much about how I feel?"

She stared at him, her chest rising and falling with each shaky breath.

And then—

"Because I miss you, Soo-ho."

His eyes widened.

"I miss us," she whispered, voice cracking. "I miss you."

For a second, she thought he was going to say something. That he was going to fix this.

But instead—

He took a step back.

His face hardened.

And the next words that left his lips shattered her completely.

"Then maybe you shouldn't have left me for him."

Ji-ae's breath caught in her throat.

A fresh wave of tears burned her eyes, but she refused to let them fall. Not in front of him. Not after that.

So she did the only thing she could do.

She turned.

And ran.

Again.

But this time—

Soo-ho didn't chase after her.

And that hurt more than anything else.

Ji-ae and Soo-ho slowly started rebuilding their friendship, falling into an easy rhythm that felt like home. Their laughter returned, their teasing banter natural, and for the first time in a while, Ji-ae felt like she had someone who truly understood her.

But Seo-jun wasn't blind.

He saw the way Ji-ae smiled more around Soo-ho, how she confided in him, how they always seemed to gravitate towards each other. And despite Ji-ae constantly reassuring him, an ugly feeling of jealousy twisted inside him.

That's when he made the biggest mistake of his life.

He cheated.

With Ju-kyung.

Ji-ae found out the next day. She didn't scream. She didn't yell. She just... shut down. Seo-jun begged, apologized, swore it was a mistake, but Ji-ae wouldn't even look at him. She avoided him completely. And when he finally cornered her, she spoke in the coldest voice he'd ever heard.

"It's over."

Seo-jun's world crumbled. But Ji-ae was already walking away.

That same day, Soo-ho found her sitting alone in the cafeteria. Without a word, he placed his tray next to hers, acting as if nothing had happened.

"You should eat," he said simply, nudging her tray toward her.

Ji-ae poked at her food absentmindedly. "I don't feel like it."

Soo-ho sighed. "You shouldn't keep everything bottled up. You need to let it out."

Ji-ae scoffed. "Let it out? And do what? Cry? Like that's going to change anything."

"It won't change what happened," Soo-ho admitted, "but it'll help *you*."

Ji-ae didn't respond. But his words stuck with her.

That evening, she found herself wandering into the park. The sky was heavy with gray clouds, the scent of rain thick in the air. She sat down on an empty bench, staring at nothing in particular. And then, just as the first raindrop hit her skin, everything came crashing down.

Suddenly, Soo-ho's voice replayed in her mind. "You shouldn't keep everything bottled up. You need to let it out."

Tears spilled from her eyes, silent at first, then uncontrollable. Her body trembled as sobs wracked through her, months of pain and heartbreak pouring out all at once.

And she wasn't alone.

Soo-ho had been there the whole time, watching from a distance. The moment he saw her shoulders shaking, he ran to her without hesitation. He didn't say a word—he just sat beside her and let her cry, offering his quiet presence as comfort.

After what felt like forever, Ji-ae, exhausted, leaned against him. Her breaths slowed, and before Soo-ho even realized it, she had fallen asleep on his shoulder.

His heart clenched. She had finally let herself feel everything, and now she was so tired that she could barely keep her eyes open. Soo-ho carefully adjusted his arms and, with gentle precision, lifted her into his arms. The rain poured harder, drenching them both, but he didn't care. He carried her all the way home.

The next morning, Ji-ae woke up feeling unusually warm. She frowned, blinking at the ceiling before sitting up. How had she gotten home?

She walked into the kitchen, rubbing her eyes. "Eomma?"

Her mother smiled knowingly. "Your friend Soo-ho carried you home in the rain last night."

Ji-ae froze, her heart skipping a beat. "He… what?"

Her mother chuckled. "He wouldn't leave until he was sure you were okay."

Ji-ae felt something stir deep inside her, something unfamiliar yet comforting.

Soo-ho had always been there.

And maybe… he always would be.

The thought lingered in Ji-ae's mind the entire morning. Soo-ho had carried her home in the rain. He had stayed. He had made sure she was okay.

Her heart felt… strange. Like it was lighter, yet somehow heavier at the same time.

But at that moment, she felt very weak. Her eyes didn't open fully even though it had been a while since she woke up. She quickly took her hand and touched her forehead.

Her mother, seeing this, quickly grabbed the thermometer from the med-kit and placed it in Ji-ae's mouth.

BEEP BEEP BEEP! (the thermometer)

"Yup. You're sick. Back to bed-"

"No! I can't be! I **NEED** to go to school today!"

"Why? You used to make an issue every time you wanted to stay at home."

"It's just-
We have an important history lesson today! Yea!"

"Nope. Back to bed."

She returned to her bedroom, quickly grabbed her phone and texted Soo-ho.

Hey. I can't come to school today...apparently I have a fever.

Soo-ho left her on read. He quickly ran to her favorite restaurant, got her favorite kimchi soup and RAN to her house.

DING-DONG!

It was Soo-ho.

Waiting anxiously to see if she was okay.

Ji-ae's mother opened the door.

"Oh Soo-ho! What a surprise! Come in!" exclaimed her mother.

As soon as Ji-ae heard his name, she rushed downstairs.

She nearly tripped over her own feet in the process, but she didn't care. When she reached the bottom of the stairs, Soo-ho stood there, slightly out of breath, holding a steaming container in his hands.

"You idiot," Ji-ae scolded, but her voice lacked any real bite. "You ran here, didn't you?"

Soo-ho rolled his eyes. "No, I *teleported.*" Then he held up the container. "I got your favorite. Thought you could use it."

Ji-ae stared at him, her heart doing something weird again—like skipping, flipping, and crashing all at once.

Her mother smiled knowingly. "I'll leave you two alone." And with that, she disappeared into the kitchen.

Ji-ae crossed her arms. "You didn't have to do this."

Soo-ho shrugged. "I wanted to."

Ji-ae sighed and plopped onto the couch. "Well, since you're already here..." She reached for the container, but Soo-ho pulled it back.

"Uh-uh," he said. "Not until you sit properly and promise to finish it."

She groaned dramatically but obeyed, sitting cross-legged. Soo-ho handed her the container, and she took a cautious sip. The warmth spread through her, comforting in a way she didn't expect.

"Better?" Soo-ho asked, watching her.

Ji-ae nodded. "Yeah."

For a moment, they just sat there in silence, the air between them oddly comfortable. Then, Soo-ho suddenly reached out and poked her forehead.

"Hey!" she protested, swatting his hand away.

"You're burning up," he said, frowning. "Maybe I should stay and take care of you."

Ji-ae blinked at him, heart racing. "What?"

Soo-ho smirked. "You heard me. I'm staying."

Ji-ae swallowed. "You're serious?"

"Dead serious." Soo-ho leaned back against the couch, completely at ease. "Now, finish your soup, sick girl."

Ji-ae huffed. "Fine, but don't start acting like my nurse or something."

Soo-ho smirked. "Too late. I'm fully prepared to be the best nurse you've ever had."

She rolled her eyes but couldn't hide the small smile tugging at her lips. She continued eating, and Soo-ho watched her closely, making sure she finished every bite. When she was done, he took the empty container and placed it on the coffee table.

"Okay, now lie down," he ordered.

Ji-ae raised a brow. "Excuse me?"

"You're sick. Rest." Soo-ho grabbed a pillow and playfully shoved it behind her. "Come on, get comfy."

Ji-ae muttered something under her breath but obeyed, lying down on the couch. Soo-ho pulled the blanket over her and sat on the floor beside her.

"Better?" he asked.

She hesitated before nodding. "Yeah."

Soo-ho grinned. "Good. Now, what do sick people do? Oh, right! Watch something dumb and fall asleep." He grabbed the TV remote. "What do you wanna watch?"

Ji-ae thought for a moment. "Something light. Maybe—"

Before she could finish, Soo-ho clicked on a random show.

"'Pororo the Little Penguin'?! Are you serious?!" Ji-ae gawked at him.

Soo-ho shrugged, biting back a laugh. "It's a classic."

"I am *not* watching this."

"Yes, you are."

"No, I'm—"

Just then, Ji-ae's mother peeked into the living room. "Oh, watching *Pororo* together? How cute."

Soo-ho smirked. "See? Your mom approves."

Ji-ae groaned, covering her face with the blanket. "This is the worst."

But as the episode played, she found herself chuckling. Soo-ho stole glances at her, feeling oddly satisfied.

A few minutes later, her eyelids grew heavy. Soo-ho noticed her breathing slow, and he couldn't help but smile. He adjusted the blanket over her and leaned back against the couch.

Just as he was about to relax, Ji-ae, half-asleep, mumbled something.

"Soo-ho..."

His breath hitched. "Yeah?"

A sleepy smile tugged at her lips. "Thanks for staying."

Soo-ho felt his heart skip, flip, and crash all at once.

"Always," he whispered.

And with that, Ji-ae drifted into peaceful sleep, completely unaware of the way Soo-ho watched over her like she was the most important person in the world.

Soo-ho stayed right where he was, sitting on the floor with his head resting against the couch, watching Ji-ae's peaceful face as she slept. Every once in a while, she mumbled something in her sleep, her nose scrunching up cutely, and Soo-ho had to fight back a chuckle.

He glanced at the clock—she had been asleep for about an hour now. He knew he should probably leave soon, but... he didn't want to.

Instead, he reached for his phone and snapped a picture.

Not to tease her with later.
Not to make fun of her.

Just... to remember this moment.

His heart felt weirdly full, and he realized something.

This—taking care of her, being here for her—felt right.

Soo-ho sighed, leaning his head back. "You're really something, Ji-ae."

As if she could hear him, Ji-ae shifted in her sleep and reached out blindly. Before he knew it, her hand landed on his.

Soo-ho froze.

Her fingers curled slightly, gripping onto him as if she didn't want him to go. His heart thumped loudly in his chest.

He should move his hand.
He *should*.

But he didn't.

Instead, he gently intertwined their fingers, squeezing her hand lightly.

Ji-ae let out a small, content sigh, snuggling deeper into the couch. Soo-ho swallowed, feeling warmth spread through him.

Then, out of nowhere—

"Mm... don't steal my banana milk..." Ji-ae murmured.

Soo-ho blinked before bursting into silent laughter. "What?"

Ji-ae frowned slightly in her sleep. "Mine..."

Soo-ho shook his head, still laughing. "Fine, fine. I won't touch your banana milk."

He let her rest a little longer before gently nudging her shoulder.

"Ji-ae," he whispered. "Wake up, sleepyhead."

Ji-ae groaned, turning away. "Five more minutes…"

"Nope," Soo-ho said, poking her cheek. "Come on, you need to drink some water."

Ji-ae peeked one eye open, glaring. "You're annoying."

Soo-ho grinned. "And yet, you're still holding my hand."

Ji-ae blinked, realizing their fingers were still intertwined.

Her face turned *red*.

She yanked her hand away, sitting up way too fast—only to wobble. Soo-ho caught her shoulders immediately.

"Whoa, take it easy," he said, steadying her.

Ji-ae groaned. "Ugh, I hate being sick."

Soo-ho smirked. "Well, I think you're kinda cute like this."

Ji-ae snapped her head toward him, eyes wide. "W-what?"

Soo-ho just shrugged, completely unfazed. "You heard me."

Ji-ae buried her face in her hands. "This is a nightmare."

Soo-ho chuckled and handed her a water bottle. "Drink, before you pass out again."

As she drank, he grabbed his phone and scrolled through his photos. Ji-ae noticed and narrowed her eyes.

"…What are you doing?"

"Oh, nothing," Soo-ho said, *very* suspiciously.

Ji-ae snatched his phone before he could react. "Wait. Did you—"

Her eyes landed on the picture he had taken of her sleeping.

Her face *exploded* into redness.

"SOO-HO!!"

Soo-ho was already laughing. "You looked cute! I had to capture the moment."

"I CAN'T BELIEVE YOU—DELETE IT!!"

"No way. I'm keeping this forever."

Ji-ae lunged at him, trying to grab his phone. Soo-ho dodged, holding it high above his head as she tried to reach for it.

"Give. It. BACK!!" she yelled, struggling.

Soo-ho smirked. "Make me."

Ji-ae *froze.*

Soo-ho immediately realized what he had just said.

Their eyes met. The air suddenly felt... different.

Neither of them moved.

Ji-ae was still half in his lap from trying to reach the phone, their faces only inches apart. Soo-ho could feel her breath against his skin, and for the first time, he panicked.

Ji-ae was the first to break the tension—by *smacking* his shoulder.

"Y-YOU IDIOT!!" She scrambled back onto the couch, face still burning.

Soo-ho cleared his throat, looking away. "Okay, okay, I'll delete it... maybe."

"*MAYBE?!*"

Soo-ho only grinned.

Ji-ae groaned and pulled the blanket over her face again. "I hate you."

"No, you don't." Soo-ho leaned back, completely relaxed.

Ji-ae peeked out from under the blanket, glaring. "How do you know?"

Soo-ho smirked, tilting his head. "Because you're still smiling."

Ji-ae immediately turned away, hiding her face.

Soo-ho just laughed.

And honestly?

He had never felt happier.

Later that evening, Soo-ho was still hanging around Ji-ae's house, much to her annoyance. (Except, was she really *that* annoyed?)

He had made himself *very* comfortable, lounging on her couch like he lived there. Ji-ae, still wrapped in her blanket, watched him suspiciously.

"Aren't you going to go home?" she asked.

"Nope," Soo-ho replied casually, scrolling through his phone.

Ji-ae groaned. "Soo-ho..."

"You're sick. Someone has to take care of you."

Ji-ae narrowed her eyes. "That's what my *mom* is for."

"She's busy," Soo-ho said, still relaxed. "So, I'm your temporary nurse."

Ji-ae rolled her eyes but secretly felt... warm.

Not because of the fever. Because of *him*.

Trying to ignore that feeling, she huffed and grabbed the remote, turning on the TV. "Fine. But I get to pick what we watch."

Soo-ho raised an eyebrow. *"As if I'd argue with a sick person."*

Ji-ae smirked in victory and put on a random K-drama. Soo-ho barely paid attention at first, but halfway through, he started getting *way* too into it.

"Why is this dude so dumb?" he suddenly blurted out.

Ji-ae looked over, amused. "Excuse me?"

"This guy," Soo-ho pointed at the male lead. "She *obviously* likes him, but he's just standing there, being all broody and clueless. If I were him, I'd just tell her."

Ji-ae tilted her head. "Tell her what?"

Soo-ho shrugged. "That I liked her."

Ji-ae blinked. "Just like that?"

"Yeah. What's the point in waiting?"

Ji-ae's heart *skipped*.

Soo-ho didn't even notice her staring. He was too busy getting annoyed at the drama, muttering under his breath about "missed chances" and "idiots in love."

Ji-ae, on the other hand, felt her brain short-circuit.

Was he talking about the drama? Or was he…?

No. No way.

She swallowed, feeling suddenly nervous.

"Then…" she started, voice quieter, "what if the girl doesn't feel the same?"

Soo-ho turned to her, as if *finally* realizing the shift in tone.

For a moment, he just looked at her.

Then, he smiled—softly.

"Then at least I'd know."

Ji-ae's breath caught.

Her fever was *definitely* not helping. Her head felt fuzzy, her heart beating faster than it should. Or maybe that was just *him*.

Before she could say anything, Soo-ho poked her forehead.

"Stop overthinking," he said, grinning. "It's just a drama."

Ji-ae scowled, swatting his hand away. "I *wasn't* overthinking."

"Sure, sure."

She glared at him, but he just laughed and ruffled her hair.

Her heart did that *weird thing* again.

And for the first time, she wondered...

Was Soo-ho really just talking about the drama?

Or was there something *more*?

After finishing her soup and resting for a while, Ji-ae still felt a bit groggy, but the warmth in her chest wasn't just from the food—it was from Soo-ho. His presence, his care, the way he looked at her like she mattered.

She stretched her arms with a little yawn. "I feel kinda stuffy."

Soo-ho looked up from his phone. "You wanna go for a walk?"

Ji-ae hesitated. "I mean... I *am* sick."

"Fresh air is good for you," he said, standing up and offering his hand. "Besides, I promise I won't let you collapse or anything. I'll carry you back if I have to."

Ji-ae rolled her eyes, but her heart thumped at the thought of him carrying her *again.* Trying to act casual, she slipped on her jacket and took his hand, ignoring how natural it felt.

The evening air was crisp, a soft breeze ruffling through Ji-ae's hair as they strolled down the quiet path near her house. Soo-ho had one hand in his pocket, the other close enough to brush against hers every few steps. Neither of them spoke much at first, just enjoying the peaceful moment.

Then, Soo-ho broke the silence. "Ji-ae."

She turned to look at him, her breath catching slightly at how serious he looked under the dim streetlights.

"What?"

He exhaled, running a hand through his hair. "I need to say something."

Ji-ae's heart pounded. "Okay..."

Soo-ho stopped walking, making her pause too. He turned to fully face her. "I've liked you for a long time."

Ji-ae's eyes widened. "W-what?"

Soo-ho let out a breathy chuckle. "I know, it's crazy, right? But I do. And I think I've always liked you, even before I realized it myself." His voice softened. "I didn't say anything because... I was scared. Scared that you'd push me away. Scared that I'd ruin what we have." He sighed. "But after everything, I don't want to keep it in anymore."

Ji-ae's mind was spinning, but her heart knew the truth before her lips could catch up.

Because she *felt* it too.

She felt it when she laughed at his stupid jokes. When she caught herself looking for him in a crowd. When he carried her home in the rain. When he showed up at her door with her favorite soup, out of breath but still smiling.

She took a shaky breath. "*Soo-ho...*"

He looked at her, eyes searching hers, waiting.

Ji-ae swallowed hard before whispering, "I like you too."

For a moment, Soo-ho just stared. Then, slowly, the biggest, happiest grin spread across his face. "Wait, really?"

Ji-ae laughed, feeling warmth rush to her cheeks. "Yes, idiot."

Soo-ho ran a hand through his hair again, clearly trying to process what just happened. "Wow. Okay. That's... wow."

Ji-ae smirked. "Are you broken?"

"Maybe," he admitted with a soft chuckle. Then, before he could stop himself, he reached out and ruffled her hair. "You're really something, Ji-ae."

She swatted his hand away, but she was grinning. "And you're annoying."

"You like me, though."

She groaned. "Regretting it already."

He laughed, and she laughed too. Their hands brushed again. This time, Soo-ho didn't hesitate—he gently took her hand in his, intertwining their fingers like it was the most natural thing in the world.

Ji-ae didn't pull away.

And maybe... she never would.

Ji-ae and Soo-ho kept walking, their fingers still laced together. The air felt lighter, the world a little warmer, even though the night breeze brushed against their skin.

"So..." Soo-ho smirked. "Now that we *both* like each other, what happens next?"

Ji-ae raised an eyebrow. "What do you mean?"

"I mean," he swung their hands playfully, "are we officially dating? Or do I have to wait for you to confess again?"

Ji-ae scoffed. "I *already* confessed, you moron."

Soo-ho grinned. "So, does that make you my girlfriend?"

Ji-ae blinked. The word sent a whole new rush of warmth through her. *His girlfriend?*

She tried to play it cool, shrugging. "I don't know... Are you going to annoy me for the rest of my life?"

"Absolutely."

"Then I guess I'm stuck with you."

Soo-ho laughed, his thumb gently brushing over her knuckles. "You *say* that like it's a bad thing."

Ji-ae rolled her eyes, but her smile gave her away.

As they walked, Soo-ho suddenly stopped and pulled her toward him.

Ji-ae yelped. "Yah! What are you—"

"Shhh," he said, putting a finger to his lips. "I have an idea."

Ji-ae eyed him suspiciously. "That's never a good thing."

Soo-ho ignored her, pointing toward the swings in the park. "Let's sit."

She narrowed her eyes. "Are you seriously making me swing when I have a fever?"

"Fresh air *and* a little fun? Sounds like a perfect cure to me."

She groaned but let him lead her to the swings anyway. He sat down first, pushing off slightly with his feet. Ji-ae followed, the chains creaking softly as she swung just enough to match his pace.

For a moment, they just enjoyed the night—the soft hum of the crickets, the distant sound of the city, the way the stars peeked through the clouds.

Then, Soo-ho spoke again, his voice softer this time. "Hey, Ji-ae?"

She turned to him, her swing slowing. "Yeah?"

He hesitated, his fingers gripping the chains tightly before finally saying, "I promise to always be here for you. No matter what."

Ji-ae's breath hitched.

She looked at him—the way his dark eyes held nothing but sincerity, the way he always managed to make her feel safe without even trying.

Without thinking, she reached out and took his hand again, squeezing it. "You already are, Soo-ho."

His lips parted slightly in surprise before a slow, happy smile spread across his face. He gave her hand a squeeze back.

And just like that, in the middle of a quiet park, under a sky full of stars, Ji-ae realized something.

Maybe love wasn't always loud or dramatic.

Maybe it was just... this.

Soft. Steady. A hand to hold on a cold night. A voice that never left, even when everything else did.

Maybe love was Soo-ho.

And maybe, just maybe...

He was hers.

Over the next few days, Ji-ae and Soo-ho grew even closer. They spent more time together—walking home, texting late at night, even studying together. And while Ji-ae still felt the sting of her breakup, with Soo-ho around, it didn't hurt *as much.*

But not everyone was happy about it.

Seo-jun watched from a distance, his jaw clenched every time he saw them together. He had lost Ji-ae once—he wasn't about to let her slip away completely.

So, he did something reckless.

One afternoon, Ji-ae was at her locker when Seo-jun suddenly appeared beside her, blocking her way.

"Can we talk?" he asked, his voice low.

Ji-ae sighed, shutting her locker. "There's nothing to talk about."

"Yes, there is." He stepped closer, his eyes pleading. "I messed up. I know that. But you and I—what we had—it was real, wasn't it?"

Ji-ae's stomach twisted. "It *was*, Seo-jun. But you ruined it."

"I'll do anything," he insisted. "I'll prove to you that I—"

"She said there's nothing to talk about."

Seo-jun stiffened. Ji-ae turned to see Soo-ho standing a few feet away, arms crossed, his usual smirk replaced by something colder.

Seo-jun scoffed. "Right. Of course, *you* show up."

Soo-ho stepped forward, placing himself between Seo-jun and Ji-ae. "You had your chance. And you blew it."

Seo-jun's eyes darkened. "You think you're any better? You think she'll choose you?"

Ji-ae grabbed Soo-ho's arm. "Let's just go."

But Seo-jun wasn't done. "You're only running to him because you're hurt, Ji-ae. But he's not the one you *really* want."

Ji-ae's breath hitched. For a second, doubt flickered in her chest.

And Soo-ho saw it.

His jaw tightened, but he didn't say anything. Instead, he just took Ji-ae's hand and walked away, leaving Seo-jun standing there, fists clenched.

That night, Ji-ae tossed and turned in bed, Seo-jun's words playing over and over in her head.

He's not the one you really want.

Was that true?

No.

Because she found her person.

The next morning, Ji-ae was feeling much better—whether it was the fresh air, Soo-ho's confession, or the fact that she'd actually gotten a full night's sleep for once, she didn't know. But one thing was certain.

Today was going to be a disaster.

Titan Academy was notorious for its *eventful* school trips. And with the people in their class? *Absolute madness was guaranteed.*

Ji-ae slung her bag over her shoulder as she walked toward the school bus. Just as she reached it, a voice called out—

"JI-AE!!!"

Before she could react, Denise tackled her into a hug.

"You're alive!" Denise gasped dramatically. "We thought you died from your fever!"

Ji-ae rolled her eyes. "It was just a fever, not the plague."

Debbie walked up, smirking. "Well, *someone* was too busy playing nurse to let us check on you." She gave Soo-ho a pointed look.

Ji-ae immediately turned to glare at him. "You told them?!"

Soo-ho shrugged, completely unbothered. "They asked why you weren't in school."

Denise wiggled her eyebrows. "Ooooh, so *boyfriend duties* came first, huh?"

Ji-ae choked. "EXCUSE ME—"

Denise and Debbie burst out laughing.

Soo-ho looked *way* too amused. "So, I'm your boyfriend now?"

Ji-ae glared at him. "Shut. Up."

Before he could tease her further, JianHao announced, clapping his hands. "Alright, everyone! Listen up! This trip is going to be a peaceful, *educational* experience."

Silence.

Then, someone coughed.

Then, Vincent *burst out laughing.*

"HAHAHA! Bro, you *really* think this class can go on a school trip without something going horribly wrong?!"

"Yeah," Zhi Kai added. "It's not a *Titan Academy* trip unless there's at least one near-death experience!"

Madeline sighed. "I give it five minutes before something explodes."

Ji-ae leaned toward Soo-ho. "Should we be worried?"

Soo-ho smirked. "Absolutely."

JianHao ignored them all and continued. "We're going to a **mountain resort for 3 days**. That means *no phones, no distractions*, and *NO causing trouble!*"

Everyone groaned.

"Ugh, no phones?" Madeline pouted. "How am I supposed to update my followers?!"

"Don't worry, Madeline. He's joking." said Ji-ae.

"More importantly," Vincent grinned, "who wants to bet on who causes the first disaster?"

Zhi Kai immediately pointed at JianHao. "It's always him."

JianHao threw his hands up. "HEY!"

Soo-ho just smirked. "At least it won't be boring."

Little did they know, the chaos was only *just* getting started.

The excitement in Class T1T5 was unreal. The school had announced a ***three-day trip to a mountain resort***, and everyone was buzzing with energy.

"FINALLY, a break from studies!" JianHao cheered, throwing his arms up.

"You don't even study," Denise muttered, rolling her eyes.

Ji-ae, meanwhile, was still processing the fact that she and Soo-ho were... something. They hadn't put a label on it yet, but ever since the walk in the park, he had been a little *too* sweet—saving a seat for her on the bus, offering her his hoodie when she was cold, and walking her to class even when it was out of his way.

Denise, Debbie, and Madeline had *noticed.*

"So," Madeline smirked, nudging Ji-ae as they waited for the bus. "Are you two official yet?"

Ji-ae's face turned red. "I—uh—"

Before she could even *try* to answer, JianHao jumped into the conversation. "Guys, guys, let's focus on the real issue here. *Who* is going to sit with *who* on the bus?"

Everyone exchanged looks.

"Oh no," Debbie muttered.

"Let's do rock-paper-scissors!" Vincent suggested.

Somehow, Ji-ae ended up sitting with Soo-ho, while JianHao got stuck with Denise (who looked like she wanted to throw him out of the window).

Soo-ho smirked. "Lucky us."

Ji-ae bit her lip. "Did you *rig* the rock-paper-scissors game?"

"Me?" Soo-ho feigned innocence. "Of course not."

JianHao groaned loudly from the seat behind them. "Can you two stop being cute? Some of us are *suffering*."

"Just admit you like Denise," Soo-ho shot back.

Denise's head snapped around. "*Excuse me?*"

JianHao coughed. "*ANYWAY.*"

A few hours into the ride, *chaos* broke loose.

- Vincent somehow convinced Debbie to play a horror game on his phone, and now she was *screaming* every five minutes.
- JianHao and Denise were *bickering* non-stop about who was taking up more space.
- Madeline was doing a *livestream* about "surviving a bus ride with crazy people."
- Ji-ae *fell asleep* on Soo-ho's shoulder, and he tried *so hard* not to move because she looked too peaceful.

By the time they arrived at the resort, everyone was *exhausted*.

The Resort and The Prank War

The resort was beautiful—lush green mountains, a lake shimmering in the distance, and cozy wooden cabins.

The teachers divided them into *boys' and girls' cabins*, but that didn't stop the chaos.

"*Guys vs. Girls PRANK WAR!*" JianHao declared the second the teachers were out of sight.

Denise smirked. "Oh, you're *on*."

That night, things *escalated*.

- The boys put toothpaste in the girls' Oreos.
- The girls filled the boys' pillows with *glitter* (which Soo-ho was *still* finding in his hair the next morning).
- Someone (*ahem* Madeline) swapped JianHao's shampoo with *green dye*.

But the *biggest* disaster happened when Ji-ae and Soo-ho were sent to *fetch firewood* for the campfire.

Ji-ae *hated* horror movies. So, when she and Soo-ho got *lost* while gathering firewood, she was *freaking out*.

"Soo-ho," she whispered. "What if there's a *ghost*?"

He chuckled. "Ji-ae, this isn't a horror movie—"

CRACK.

A branch snapped behind them. Ji-ae *screamed* and immediately *latched onto Soo-ho.*

Soo-ho stiffened. "Okay. That was... cute."

Ji-ae realized what she was doing and *jumped back, flustered.* "S-Sorry!"

Soo-ho just smiled, ruffling her hair. "You're adorable when you're scared."

"I am *not*—"

"Ji-ae." His voice softened. "Do you... ever think about us?"

Ji-ae's heart pounded. "W-What do you mean?"

Soo-ho hesitated before taking her hands in his. "But I don't want to rush you. So... just tell me when you're ready."

Ji-ae felt warmth spread through her chest.

"Of course I already am. Soo-ho, it's weird to say this, but...you're my boyfriend now."

Soo-ho's smile was so bright it could've rivaled the campfire waiting for them back at the resort.

And just like that, under the moonlit sky, *they weren't just "something" anymore. They were everything.*

After finally making it back to the camp, Ji-ae and Soo-ho thought the drama was over. *They were wrong.*

The second they stepped into the campfire area, all eyes were on them.

"There you are!" Denise huffed. "What took you so long? *Wait... were you two alone?*"

JianHao smirked. "Ohhh, were you guys having a *moment?*"

Ji-ae turned red. "N-No! We just got lost—"

Madeline gasped dramatically. "Lost *in the woods? At night?* Soo-ho, did you *save* her?"

Soo-ho chuckled, but before he could answer, Vincent said, "If this was a drama, this would be the *episode before the confession.*"

Ji-ae: *...WELL.*

Things were *fine* until the next day. The teachers announced a *hiking trip to the waterfall,* and that's when the *real* drama started.

Enter *Jayden*.

Jayden was from Class N4T1, and he was known for being annoyingly charming. *And* apparently, he had taken an interest in Ji-ae.

While they were hiking, Jayden suddenly appeared next to her. "Hey, Ji-ae, right? You're new here."

Ji-ae blinked. "Uh, yeah?"

"I saw you at the campfire last night," he continued, flashing a grin. "You're cute."

Ji-ae nearly tripped.

Soo-ho, walking right behind them, *heard everything*. His eyes *narrowed*.

Jayden, completely oblivious, kept talking. "Since you're new, how about I show you around the school sometime? Maybe we could get some coffee?"

Ji-ae awkwardly laughed. "I—uh—"

Before she could answer, Soo-ho *casually* stepped between them, throwing an arm around Ji-ae's shoulders.

"Actually," Soo-ho said coolly, "she's already got someone for that."

Ji-ae's face heated up. "Soo-ho—"

Jayden raised an eyebrow. "Oh? And who would that be?"

Soo-ho smirked. "Me."

Silence. *Complete silence.* Even the birds in the trees seemed to pause.

JianHao, who had been watching everything, whispered to Denise, *"Did he just drop the bomb?"*

Denise whispered back, *"I think he did."*

Jayden's smirk faltered. "Oh… I see. Well, that's interesting."

Before leaving, he shot a glance at Ji-ae and said, "Let me know if you change your mind."

Ji-ae groaned. *Why did this feel like a bad K-drama episode?*

The hike ended at a beautiful waterfall. The water was crystal clear, and a few students started jumping in.

Madeline pulled out her phone. "Alright, who wants to make a viral video?"

Before anyone could answer, JianHao and Vincent *pushed Denise into the water.*

"YOU'RE DEAD!" she shrieked, splashing wildly.

Meanwhile, Soo-ho and Ji-ae were sitting on a rock, watching the chaos unfold.

"Are you okay?" Soo-ho asked.

Ji-ae sighed. "I think Jayden's just... messing around, but it's still annoying."

Soo-ho frowned. "If he bothers you again, let me know."

Ji-ae smiled. "Protective, are we?"

Soo-ho smirked. "Only when it comes to you."

Before Ji-ae could respond, a *LOUD scream* echoed through the area.

Everyone turned to see *JianHao slipping on a rock—and falling straight into the water.*

"*MY PHONE!*" he shrieked. "MY PRECIOUS PHONE!"

Denise doubled over laughing. "*Karma, baby!*"

Madeline, still recording, gasped. "*THIS IS GOLD!*"

The teachers, now *completely done* with life, announced that it was *time to go back.*

That night, the students gathered around the bonfire. Someone suggested playing *Truth or Dare*, and that's when the *final* drama of the trip unfolded.

When it was Soo-ho's turn, JianHao smirked. "Truth or dare?"

Soo-ho leaned back. "Dare."

JianHao grinned. "I dare you... to confess to the person you like."

Silence. *Absolute silence.*

Ji-ae's *heart stopped.*

Denise nudged her. "Ohhh, it's happening."

Soo-ho, unfazed, simply turned to Ji-ae and said, "I already did."

Ji-ae froze. "W-What?"

Soo-ho smirked. "When we got lost in the woods."

Madeline gasped. *"OH MY GOSH, IT'S TRUE?!"*

Debbie clapped. "FINALLY."

Denise raised an eyebrow. "Ji-ae, what's your response?"

Ji-ae, flustered beyond belief, took a deep breath before softly saying, "I already answered."

JianHao groaned. "YOU TWO HAVE BEEN DATING THIS WHOLE TIME?! I FEEL BETRAYED!"

The whole class *exploded* in shock.

Vincent shook his head. "This wasn't Truth or Dare. This was *a drama finale.*"

Ji-ae, red-faced, hid her face in Soo-ho's shoulder. "I *hate* you for this."

Soo-ho chuckled, wrapping an arm around her. "You love me."

Ji-ae muttered, "...Maybe."

And that night, under the stars, Kang Ji-ae and Lee Soo-ho's story truly began—not just as friends, but as *something more.*

The school trip had been chaotic, but nothing could have prepared Ji-ae and Soo-ho for the drama that awaited them back at Titan Academy.

The *moment* Ji-ae stepped into the classroom, she could feel everyone's eyes on her. Whispers filled the air.

"She's dating Lee Soo-ho? *No way.*"
"I thought Soo-ho didn't care about anyone?"
"Didn't Jayden try to hit on her? This is getting interesting."

Ji-ae sighed and slumped into her seat. "I hate this."

Denise smirked. "You *did* confess in front of the whole class. What did you expect?"

Madeline plopped down next to her, scrolling through her phone. "Wanna know what's worse? Someone *posted it* on Titan Academy's gossip page."

Ji-ae's eyes widened. "WHAT?!"

Madeline turned her phone around. Sure enough, a post read:

"Breaking News: Cold-Hearted Lee Soo-ho Finally Falls for a Girl—Who Is She?!"

The comments were *even worse.*

- *No way Soo-ho actually likes someone.*
- *I give them a month.*
- *Jayden should've been faster LOL.*

Ji-ae groaned. "This is a nightmare."

At that moment, Soo-ho walked into class. The room *fell silent.*

He blinked, confused, then spotted Ji-ae. Walking over, he casually leaned against her desk.

"Hey."

Ji-ae buried her face in her arms. "Kill me."

Soo-ho chuckled. "What happened now?"

Denise handed him Madeline's phone. He skimmed the post and *laughed.*

"Oh. This is nothing."

Ji-ae glared at him. "*Nothing?* My life is *ruined!*"

JianHao, appearing out of nowhere, slung an arm around Soo-ho. "So, how does it feel to be Titan Academy's newest power couple?"

Soo-ho smirked. "I don't mind."

Ji-ae: *WHY IS HE SO CALM?!*

Meanwhile, Jayden, sitting in the back, watched the whole exchange, his expression unreadable.Lunch was supposed to be peaceful. But then, Jayden slid into the seat across from Ji-ae, smirking.

"Hey, Ji-ae."

Soo-ho, sitting beside her, immediately tensed.

Ji-ae forced a polite smile. "Uh... hi?"

Jayden tilted his head. "So, you and Soo-ho, huh? That's... unexpected."

Ji-ae shifted uncomfortably. "Yeah...?"

Jayden leaned in slightly. "You sure about that choice?"

Soo-ho's *chair scraped against the floor* as he leaned forward. "What's your problem?"

Jayden chuckled. "Relax, man. Just making conversation."

Soo-ho's jaw clenched. "No, you're trying to start something."

The air around them *turned tense*. Students were *watching*.

Denise whispered to Madeline, "Are we about to witness a fight?"

Madeline whispered back, "If we do, I'm recording."

Before things could get worse, Ji-ae *grabbed Soo-ho's hand* under the table, squeezing it.

Soo-ho glanced at her. Ji-ae shook her head slightly.

After a moment, Soo-ho sighed and leaned back. "Stay out of our business, Jayden."

Jayden smirked. "Sure, sure. For now."

Then he left.

Ji-ae let out a breath. "That was *stressful*."

Soo-ho looked at her. "If he bothers you again, tell me."

Denise grinned. "Look at you, all *protective boyfriend mode*."

Ji-ae groaned. "Don't start."

JianHao clapped his hands. "Alright! Let's all focus on the real issue here—how do we milk this drama for entertainment?"

Madeline: "I vote for making a fake love triangle storyline and selling it to the gossip page."

Ji-ae: "*PLEASE NO.*"

But something told Ji-ae… this drama was *far from over.*

It all started when Ji-ae opened her locker and found a neatly folded letter inside.

Denise, standing beside her, gasped. "Is that… a *love letter?*"

Ji-ae blinked. "Huh?"

Madeline snatched it before Ji-ae could react. "Let's see… 'To the most beautiful girl in Titan Academy…' *OH HO!*"

JianHao, appearing out of nowhere, gasped dramatically. "*Scandalous!*"

Soo-ho, who had just walked up, frowned. "What's that?"

Denise grinned. "Someone has a *secret admirer.*"

Soo-ho's eyes *narrowed.* "What?"

Ji-ae groaned, grabbing the letter back. "It's probably just a prank—"

Vincent read over her shoulder. "There's no name. Just 'Your Secret Admirer.'"

Madeline gasped. "This is *peak drama.*"

JianHao: "Soo-ho, how do you feel about this?"

Soo-ho: *Death glare activated.*

The next day, Titan Academy's gossip page had a *new* post:

"Lee Soo-ho's Girlfriend Caught in a Love Triangle? Who is the Mystery Admirer?"

Ji-ae nearly *threw* her phone across the room. "WHO IS POSTING THESE?!"

Soo-ho, completely unamused, muttered, "I don't like this."

Denise, laughing, said, "This is *hilarious.*"

JianHao added, "But also, we *must* investigate."

Madeline grinned. "A school-wide *mystery*! The plot thickens!"

Ji-ae sighed. "I hate all of you."

One day, Ji-ae was taking a walk in the park. As she sat down on a bench, Seo-jun spotted her. He sat down next to her and tried to start a conversation.

"Hey! Whatcha doin' nowadays?"

Ji-ae sighed. "What are you doing here? Isn't Ju-kyung looking for you?"

"No. Plus, I think we need to talk. I wanted to clear things up between us."

"Fine. What do you wanna talk about?"

"I just wanted to say..that...I'm not mad that you're dating Soo-ho. Not that I should have an opinion on that, but, I just thought you should know."

"Wow. Thats actually really nice of you, Seo-jun."

They smiled at each other. Then Ji-ae looked at her phone.

"Woah! It's late. I'll see you tomorrow. Byeee!!"

"Bye!"

Things between Seo-jun and Ji-ae had changed. They became best friends.

But to add to the school drama that was happening in the background, Ji-ae and Soo-ho got detention after being *framed* for something they *didn't* do.

Teacher: "You both *skipped class* yesterday, didn't you?"

Ji-ae: "NO?! We were literally in the library—"

Soo-ho: "Check the security cameras."

Teacher: "Oh... Well w-we don't have those in the library!"

Ji-ae: "..."

Soo-ho: "…"

Teacher: "Detention. 3 hours."

Ji-ae: *THIS SCHOOL IS A JOKE.*

Somehow, detention *got worse* when the teacher *forgot they were there* and *locked the door on his way out.*

Ji-ae banged on the door. "HELLO?! YOU FORGOT US?!"

Soo-ho sighed. "Unbelievable."

Ji-ae groaned and sat down. "Great. Just *great.*"

Soo-ho smirked. "At least I'm here."

Ji-ae rolled her eyes. "Oh wow, lucky me."

Soo-ho chuckled, leaning back. "You love me."

Ji-ae muttered, "Unfortunately."

Soo-ho smirked. "I heard that."

Ji-ae: "*Good.*"

They sat in comfortable silence for a moment until Soo-ho suddenly said, "By the way, I'm finding out who wrote that letter."

Ji-ae blinked. "It doesn't matter."

Soo-ho looked at her. "It does to me."

Her heart skipped a beat.

Okay...maybe getting locked in wasnt so bad.

Ji-ae had been *fine* at first. But as time passed and the realization sank in that they were *trapped*, something inside her started to crack.

The room felt *smaller*. The air felt *thicker*.

Her breathing turned shallow.

Soo-ho noticed immediately. "Ji-ae?"

She was staring at the door, her hands trembling.

Soo-ho sat up. "Ji-ae. Look at me."

She shook her head, tears brimming in her eyes. "I-I can't— I feel like— I can't breathe—"

Soo-ho's heart *dropped*.

He *moved fast*, kneeling in front of her and taking her hands. "Hey, hey. You're okay. I'm right here."

She gasped, struggling to get air. "We—we're stuck. What if no one— what if—"

Soo-ho gently cupped her face, forcing her to meet his eyes. "Breathe with me, Ji-ae. Just focus on me."

He took a slow, deep breath. "In."

Ji-ae tried to follow, but her breath hitched. A tear slipped down her cheek.

Soo-ho wiped it away, his voice *softer* than she'd ever heard it. "Again. In."

She tried again. This time, she inhaled shakily.

"Good," he murmured. "Now out."

She exhaled.

Soo-ho gave her a reassuring nod. "Again."

Slowly, she followed his rhythm, her breaths becoming steadier.

After a while, her hands stopped trembling.

Ji-ae let out a weak laugh. "That... was embarrassing."

Soo-ho frowned. "It wasn't."

She wiped her eyes. "I just— I hate being locked up. It reminds me of—" She stopped herself.

Soo-ho studied her quietly. "You don't have to talk about it."

She swallowed hard. "Thanks... for helping."

He sighed and sat beside her. "You don't need to thank me."

For a moment, there was silence. Then, Soo-ho quietly said, "I'll never let you be stuck alone again."

Ji-ae turned to look at him, her heart pounding.

"...Soo-ho."

Before she could say more, they suddenly heard a *click*.

The door *swung open*.

"THERE YOU GUYS ARE!"

JianHao stood there, out of breath, with Denise and Madeline behind him.

Ji-ae and Soo-ho quickly *moved apart*.

Denise smirked. "Oooh, were we interrupting something?"

Ji-ae turned *red*. "NO."

JianHao grinned. "Whatever you say... *lovebirds*."

Ji-ae groaned. "I *hate* all of you."

But as they walked out, Soo-ho's hand *brushed* against hers.

And this time... she didn't pull away.

Ji-ae *thought* the worst was over after being locked in a classroom.

She was wrong.

It started when Ji-ae noticed Soo-ho texting *a lot.*

During class. In the hallways. At lunch.

And every time she tried to peek, he'd *turn his phone away.*

Ji-ae: *Suspicious.*

Denise: *Scandalous.*

Madeline: *DUMP HIM.*

JianHao: *Let's investigate.*

Ji-ae tried to play it cool. She wasn't *jealous.* Definitely not. Nope. Not at all.

Until she caught a glimpse of a message.

Unknown Number:*Can't wait to see you again, Soo-ho* ♥?

Ji-ae: *EXCUSE ME?!*

Ji-ae *stormed* up to Soo-ho in the cafeteria.

"Soo-ho," she said sweetly. *Too sweetly.* "Who are you texting?"

Soo-ho barely looked up. "No one."

Ji-ae smiled. "Ohhh, really? Then why is some *mystery person* texting you hearts?!"

Soo-ho blinked. "...What?"

JianHao and Denise *watched like hawks.*

Soo-ho sighed. "Ji-ae, it's not what you—"

Before he could explain, Debbie *appeared out of nowhere* and *tripped,* spilling an entire tray of noodles on him.

The whole cafeteria went *silent.*

Ji-ae *choked* on laughter.

Soo-ho, covered in sauce, closed his eyes. "I hate this school."

JianHao stood dramatically. "THE UNIVERSE HAS SPOKEN."

Madeline gasped. "IT'S A SIGN."

Denise smirked. "Ji-ae, now's your chance to *grill* him."

Ji-ae tried *so hard* not to laugh. "Okay, okay, Soo-ho, who was texting you?"

Soo-ho groaned. "It's a surprise—"

Madeline: "FOR WHO?! THAT MYSTERY PERSON?!"

Soo-ho sighed. "For *you,* Ji-ae."

The table went silent.

Ji-ae blinked. "Me?"

Soo-ho, still covered in noodles, muttered, "Yes. I was planning a surprise for you, but *clearly*, that's ruined now."

Ji-ae turned *red*. "Oh."

JianHao whispered, "*AWKWARD.*"

Denise grinned. "So... Ji-ae, what do you have to say for *accusing* your loving boyfriend?"

Ji-ae mumbled, "Sorry."

Soo-ho smirked. "Louder?"

Ji-ae groaned. "I SAID SORRY."

The cafeteria *cheered*.

Ji-ae buried her face in her hands. *I hate my life.*

Soo-ho, still smirking, leaned in and whispered, "You were jealous, weren't you?"

Ji-ae shoved a napkin at him. "Just clean yourself, loser."

Just when Ji-ae thought things couldn't get worse, a *new post* popped up on the school gossip page.

BREAKING NEWS: JI-AE AND SOO-HO'S LOVER'S QUARREL—IS THEIR RELATIONSHIP IN TROUBLE?!

The post included:

1. A *zoomed-in* picture of Ji-ae looking mad.
2. Soo-ho covered in noodles.
3. A *dramatic* caption: **"Is this the end?"**

Ji-ae: *I'M GOING TO SCREAM.*

Soo-ho: *I give up on this school.*

JianHao: *I love this school.*

Madeline: *We have to keep the drama alive.*

Denise: *So when's the wedding?*

Ji-ae: *…I hate all of you.*

Ji-ae had *had enough.*

The gossip page was out of control. Her *relationship* was now the school's *favorite drama series.* And worst of all?

SOMEONE WAS SELLING "TEAM SOO-HO" AND "TEAM JI-AE" SHIRTS.

JianHao, Denise, and Madeline stood in front of Ji-ae and Soo-ho, holding up two shirts.

"Team Soo-ho ♥?" (with an *edited* picture of Soo-ho *dramatically sad* in his noodle-covered state).

"Team Ji-ae ?" (with a *zoomed-in* image of her looking *angry* in the cafeteria).

Ji-ae stared. "WHAT. IS. THIS."

JianHao grinned. "Capitalism."

Denise nodded. "We're making *so much* money."

Madeline smirked. "We're selling out fast. Mostly 'Team Soo-ho,' though."

Ji-ae gasped. "EXCUSE ME?!"

Soo-ho smirked. "As expected."

Ji-ae glared. "YOU THINK THIS IS FUNNY?"

Soo-ho shrugged. "A little."

Ji-ae snatched a *Team Soo-ho* shirt and *threw* it at his face. "I HATE YOU."

Denise grinned. "Ooooh, that's *great* promo for 'Team Ji-ae.'"

JianHao nodded. "We should make *stickers* next."

Ji-ae: *I am surrounded by idiots.*

Meanwhile, Soo-ho was *still* determined to find the person behind the gossip page.

"I *swear* I'll catch them," he muttered.

Ji-ae raised an eyebrow. "Why do you care so much?"

Soo-ho looked at her. "Because they keep making you upset."

Ji-ae blinked.

JianHao appeared. "What if the gossip page person is among us?"

Madeline gasped. "*PLOT TWIST!*"

Denise smirked. "I bet it's Vincent."

Ji-ae: "That... actually makes sense."

Soo-ho: "Let's interrogate him."

Ji-ae: ...*Oh no.*

Ji-ae, Soo-ho, JianHao, Denise, and Madeline *cornered* Vincent after class.

JianHao: *slams hands on desk* "TALK."

Vincent: "What?"

Denise: "We *know* you run the gossip page."

Vincent: "No, I don't."

Madeline: "THEN WHO DOES?!"

Vincent: "How would *I* know?"

Soo-ho: *intense stare* "You posted that picture of me, didn't you?"

Vincent: "...Which one?"

Ji-ae: "THE NOODLE ONE."

Vincent *laughed*. "Oh yeah, that was funny."

Soo-ho: *death glare intensifies*

Ji-ae: "SO IT *WAS* YOU?!"

Vincent: "No, but I *might* know who it is."

Everyone: *GASPS*

Ji-ae grabbed his shirt. "WHO?!"

Vincent smirked. "Make me an offer."

Ji-ae: "I WILL END YOU."

Soo-ho: *cracks knuckles* "I second that."

JianHao: "Can I record this?"

Denise: "Do it."

Madeline: "This is *gold*."

Ji-ae: "GUYS, FOCUS."

Vincent: "Alright, alright! I *heard* the gossip page person is someone... *unexpected*."

Ji-ae: "WHO?!"

Vincent smirked. "Wouldn't you like to know."

Ji-ae: *I AM GOING TO LOSE MY MIND.*

Ji-ae and Soo-ho had **one goal**: *Expose the gossip page mastermind.*

But first, they needed a plan.

Mission: "Find the Rat"

Ji-ae slammed a notebook on the table. "Alright, we need suspects."

Denise scribbled names down. "Let's see... Vincent is shady."

Madeline nodded. "But *too* obvious."

JianHao leaned forward. "What if it's... **Principal Loh**?"

Soo-ho: "Be serious."

Ji-ae: "Actually, that *would* be hilarious."

JianHao: *writing furiously* "Plot twist... Principal Loh is secretly a drama queen."

Denise rolled her eyes. "Okay, real suspects?"

Ji-ae thought hard. "It has to be someone who's *always* around, but sneaky enough to stay hidden."

Soo-ho leaned back. "Then we need bait."

Madeline gasped. "Ooooh! FAKE SCANDAL TIME."

Ji-ae and Soo-ho exchanged looks.

Ji-ae: "I hate this."

Soo-ho: "I *love* this."

Step 1: The Fake Breakup

Denise grabbed her phone. "Alright, let's make it dramatic."

JianHao: *fake sobbing* "I CAN'T BELIEVE THEY'RE OVER."

Madeline: "SOO-HO WAS SPOTTED WITH ANOTHER GIRL."

Denise: "JI-AE WAS SEEN CRYING IN THE BATHROOM."

Ji-ae: *fake gasps* "WHO SPREAD SUCH A RUMOR?!"

Soo-ho: *smirks* "Oh no, my reputation."

Denise hit *post*. **BOOM.** The school went WILD.

Within *minutes*, the gossip page posted:

BREAKING: JI-AE AND SOO-HO—IS THIS THE END?!

SOURCE SAYS THERE WAS TEARS! ANOTHER GIRL?!

Ji-ae: "GOT THEM."

Soo-ho: "Now we wait."

Step 2: The Trap

JianHao *accidentally* left a fake notebook labeled **"TOP SECRET: WHO I LIKE"** in the library.

Inside? A fake letter saying **Ji-ae secretly had a crush on JianHao.**

Denise: "That is *so* evil."

Madeline: "I love it."

Ji-ae: "WHY AM I THE TARGET?!"

Soo-ho: "It's for the mission, babe."

Ji-ae: *glare.* "Did you just call me—"

Soo-ho: *walks away.*

***Step 3*: GOTCHA.**

That night, the gossip page posted again.

NEW UPDATE: LOVE TRIANGLE?! JI-AE AND JIANHAO?!

Ji-ae: *DEEP INHALE.*

Soo-ho: "Found them."

Ji-ae: "WHO?!"

Soo-ho smirked, turning his phone around. **An IP address. A classroom number.**

Ji-ae's eyes widened.

Denise: "Wait... that's—"

JianHao: "OH. MY. GOSH."

Madeline gasped. "THE BETRAYAL."

Soo-ho grinned. "Let's go catch them in the act."

The culprit was in Classroom N4T1.

Ji-ae and Soo-ho **stormed** in, followed by their squad. Denise had her phone *ready to record*, Madeline looked *way too excited*, and JianHao whispered, "This is the best day of my life."

And there, sitting at a desk, typing on their phone...

...WAS VINCENT.

Ji-ae: "I *knew* it!"

Vincent: *blinks.* "What."

Soo-ho: "WE CAUGHT YOU, TRAITOR."

Vincent: "Caught me *what*? I'm literally playing Candy Crush."

Ji-ae: *pauses.* "...Oh."

Denise: "Wait, so *he's not* the one?"

Vincent: "Of course not! I don't care about your *drama*. I just enjoy watching it."

JianHao: "Fair."

Madeline sighed. "Dang. Who *is* it, then?"

Soo-ho checked his phone again. "The signal came from *this room*, though."

Ji-ae looked around. "Who else is even *in here*?"

Then, in the corner...

A shadow moved.

JianHao gasped. "A GHOST?!"

Madeline: "WE NEED AN EXORCIST."

Denise: "Or maybe it's just a *person*, you idiots."

Everyone turned.

The person stood up, revealing themselves.

IT WAS... ALEX.

Ji-ae: *confused.* "Who?"

Soo-ho: *also confused.* "Who?"

Denise: *more confused.* "WHO?!"

Alex sighed. "I'M IN YOUR CLASS."

Madeline gasped. "OH MY GOSH, BACKGROUND CHARACTER TURNED VILLAIN."

Ji-ae: "WHY WOULD YOU DO THIS?!"

Alex crossed his arms. "Because it's *funny*."

Soo-ho: "YOU RUINED MY LIFE FOR FUN?!"

Alex shrugged. "And for the *views*."

Denise: "Wait... you *made money* off this?!"

Alex grinned. "Sponsors, baby."

JianHao: "Respect."

Ji-ae: "DON'T *RESPECT* HIM."

Soo-ho: "DELETE. EVERYTHING. NOW."

Alex sighed dramatically. "Fine."

Alex *reluctantly* shut down the gossip page. The school *went into mourning* because now they had *no tea to sip.*

But Ji-ae and Soo-ho?

Finally, some *peace.*

Until—

Denise: "So... what if *we* started our own gossip page?"

JianHao: *grinning* "BRILLIANT."

Ji-ae: "NO."

Soo-ho: "ABSOLUTELY NOT."

Madeline: "Too late, we already made an account."

Ji-ae and Soo-ho: "WE HATE YOU ALL."

The End... for now.

Just when Ji-ae and Soo-ho thought they could finally enjoy a normal day...

BOOM.

A new announcement appeared on the school board.

"WELCOME TO TITAN ACADEMY'S MYSTERY CHALLENGE! WINNER GETS A SECRET PRIZE!"

Madeline: "Oooooh, mystery prize!"

Denise: "We *have* to win."

JianHao: "I bet it's something *life-changing*."

Soo-ho: "Or detention."

Ji-ae sighed. "I am NOT getting involved in another—"

Suddenly, a voice echoed through the speakers:

"ATTENTION! EVERYONE IS NOW PART OF THE MYSTERY CHALLENGE. YOU HAVE NO CHOICE."

Ji-ae: "ARE YOU KIDDING ME?!"

Soo-ho: "I *hate* this school."

But what IS the challenge? What chaos awaits? And will Ji-ae and Soo-ho survive another round of Titan Academy madness?!

The entire school erupted in chaos.

Students ran around, *demanding answers*. Teachers looked just as *confused*.

Principal Loh appeared over the loudspeaker again.

"ALL STUDENTS MUST COMPLETE THE CHALLENGES TO UNLOCK THE FINAL PRIZE. GOOD LUCK."

Then the announcement cut off.

Ji-ae: "What *kind* of challenge?!"

Soo-ho: "Knowing this school? Probably *psychological warfare*."

JianHao: "Or something *deadly*."

Madeline: "I *hope* it's deadly."

Denise: "You need help."

Then, a loud *ding* on their phones.

A new message appeared:

"Challenge 1: FIND THE MYSTERY TEACHER HIDING IN THE SCHOOL. FIRST TO DO SO GETS A CLUE FOR THE FINAL PRIZE."

Ji-ae: "Okay, how hard can it be to find a teacher?"

Madeline: "Very. They probably disguised themselves as a *student*."

JianHao: "Or a *locker*."

Denise: "Be *serious*, guys."

Soo-ho smirked. "Or what if they're *hiding in plain sight?*"

Everyone turned to look at Vincent.

Vincent: "Why are you all looking at me?"

Ji-ae: "Are *you* the teacher?"

Vincent: "I'M SIXTEEN."

Students **rampaged** through the school.

- Debbie **flipped a desk** trying to find the teacher.
- JianHao **interrogated the janitor**.
- Denise **dragged** Principal Loh out of his office, screaming, "ARE YOU THE TEACHER?!"
- Madeline... *set a fire alarm off* to "flush them out."

Ji-ae and Soo-ho?

They just stood there. Watching. **Regretting everything.**

Ji-ae: "This school is a mental asylum."

Soo-ho: "And we're the inmates."

Finally, a **scream** rang out from the cafeteria.

JianHao: "THE TEACHER IS HERE!"

Everyone **rushed in**—and saw...

The lunch lady.

Ji-ae: "Wait... MRS. LIM IS THE TEACHER?!"

Mrs. Lim: *taking off her apron* "Surprise."

Soo-ho: "What the—"

Before anyone could react, Principal Loh's voice came back.

"CONGRATULATIONS! YOU HAVE COMPLETED CHALLENGE 1. PREPARE FOR CHALLENGE 2."

Ji-ae: "No. NO. I'M *DONE*."

Soo-ho: "Too bad. We're trapped in this nightmare."

The lights in the school **flickered off**.

A blood-red message appeared on the digital boards.

"CHALLENGE 2: ESCAPE THE HAUNTED SCHOOL. LAST TEAM STANDING GETS THE NEXT CLUE."

Denise: *panicking* "HAUNTED?! WHAT DO YOU MEAN *HAUNTED?!*"

JianHao: "OH NO. WE'RE IN A HORROR MOVIE."

Madeline: "THIS. IS. AMAZING."

Ji-ae: *deadpan* "I am going to lose my mind."

Soo-ho: *grinning* "This is getting interesting."

The entire school was *pitch black.*

Only the **red emergency lights** flickered.

A robotic voice echoed through the halls.

"SURVIVE UNTIL DAWN. DON'T GET CAUGHT."

Ji-ae: **"I REFUSE TO PLAY THIS GAME."**

Soo-ho: **"We literally have no choice."**

JianHao: *excitedly* "Guys, I *love* horror movies."

Denise: "THIS ISN'T A MOVIE! THIS IS REAL LIFE."

Madeline: "Okay, but if someone gets possessed, can I record it?"

Ji-ae: "Madeline, I *swear—*"

A screen lit up, displaying the *official* rules:

1. The school is now a **haunted maze.**
2. There are **ghosts** roaming the halls.
3. If a ghost **touches you**, you're out.
4. **Last team standing wins the next clue.**

Ji-ae: *horrified* "There are *actual ghosts*?!"

Denise: "NOPE. NOPE. NOPE."

JianHao: "Relax, it's probably just teachers in costumes."

Right then—

A BLOODCURDLING SCREAM RIPPED THROUGH THE HALLS.

Denise: *freaking out* "WHAT WAS THAT?!"

JianHao: *not so brave anymore* "I HAVE REGRETS."

Ji-ae grabbed Soo-ho's arm. "We are *not* splitting up. That's how people **die** in horror movies."

Soo-ho: *grinning* "Scared, Ji-ae?"

Ji-ae: "I WILL LEAVE YOU FOR DEAD."

Denise: "Okay, listen, we need a *plan*."

Madeline: "Or we just run around and scream."

Ji-ae: "That's the worst idea ever."

JianHao: "I like it."

Suddenly—

A **shadow** appeared at the end of the hallway.

Tall. Dark. **NOT MOVING.**

Denise: "Nope. Nope. NOPE."

Madeline: *excited* "I'M GOING TO POKE IT."

Ji-ae: "WHAT IS WRONG WITH YOU?!"

Before anyone could stop her—

Madeline **threw her shoe** at it.

The shadow MOVED.

THEN STARTED RUNNING.

JianHao: "OH MY GOSH IT'S REAL, RUNNNN—"

Screaming. Absolute chaos. EVERYONE ran for their lives.

As they ran, Denise *tripped.*

Denise: "GUYS, HELP—"

Ji-ae: "I'M SORRY, BUT YOU'RE ON YOUR OWN."

Soo-ho: "JI-AE."

Denise: "YOU TRAITORS."

The shadow **closed in on her.**

Denise: *panicking* "PLEASE, I'M TOO PRETTY TO DIE—"

The shadow **reached out—**

And...

Tapped her shoulder.

A loud *BEEP* sounded.

Denise's phone screen flashed:

"YOU ARE OUT."

Denise: *gasping for breath* "I hate. This. School."

Ji-ae: "Okay. New plan. We throw JianHao as bait."

JianHao: "EXCUSE ME?!"

Soo-ho: "I support this idea."

JianHao: "BETRAYAL."

Just then—

More shadows appeared.

The ghosts were **closing in.**

Ji-ae grabbed Soo-ho's hand.

Ji-ae: "RUN, YOU IDIOTS."

And so, **the horror survival game continued...**

The ghosts were **everywhere.**

Soo-ho and Ji-ae sprinted down the hallway, dragging JianHao and Madeline behind them.

Denise was already *eliminated*, sitting grumpily in the corner while the ghosts walked past her.

Denise: *muttering* "At least I don't have to run anymore."

JianHao: *panting* "Why... is... every... school event... so... PHYSICALLY DEMANDING?!"

Madeline: "I'm actually having *so much fun*."

Ji-ae: "THERE IS SOMETHING *SERIOUSLY* WRONG WITH YOU."

They turned a corner and **froze**.

The hallway was **blocked off**—only one way out.

Ji-ae: "Okay. Soo-ho, what do we do?"

Soo-ho: "Hmm. Let's think logically."

JianHao: "OR—hear me out—we just start SCREAMING."

Ji-ae: "That is the dumbest—"

Before she could finish, the lights **flickered**.

A **ghost** appeared **RIGHT BEHIND THEM.**

Ji-ae: "OH MY—"

Madeline: "HIT IT!"

Ji-ae: "WHAT?!"

Madeline: "I DON'T KNOW, MAYBE IT WORKS."

JianHao: *grabbing Ji-ae's arm* "JI-AE, YOU'RE THE FASTEST, GO!"

Ji-ae had no choice. She **grabbed Soo-ho's hand** and **sprinted**.

Straight into—

A DEAD END.

Ji-ae: *panicking* "WE'RE TRAPPED. WE'RE GOING TO DIE."

Soo-ho: "I don't think they can actually *kill* us—"

JianHao: *grabs Ji-ae's shoulders* "I'm sorry, Ji-ae."

Ji-ae: "...What?"

JianHao: **SHOVES HER FORWARD.**

Ji-ae: **"JIANHAO YOU TRAITOR—"**

BEEP!

Ji-ae's phone screen flashed.

"YOU ARE OUT."

Ji-ae: **"YOU LITTLE—"**

JianHao: "I HAD TO DO IT, I'M SORRY."

Soo-ho: **"YOU SACRIFICED MY GIRLFRIEND?!"**

JianHao: *guilty smile* "For survival?"

Madeline: "Honestly, I respect it."

Ji-ae: *death glaring* "I hope the ghosts GET YOU."

JianHao: *nervously laughing* "Haha... yeah, okay, we should probably RUN."

The remaining students were down to just a few teams.

Ji-ae sat with Denise and the other eliminated students, **plotting revenge.**

Ji-ae: "If Soo-ho doesn't avenge me, I'm dumping him."

Denise: "Ooooh, drama. I support."

Meanwhile, Soo-ho **locked eyes with the final ghost.**

Only he, JianHao, and Madeline were left.

Winner gets the next clue.

Madeline: *smirking* "I have an idea."

Soo-ho: "What?"

Madeline: "Run straight at the ghost and scare IT."

JianHao: **"MADNESS."**

Soo-ho: "You know what? Let's try it."

Ji-ae: **"EXCUSE ME?!"**

And then, to *everyone's* shock—

Soo-ho CHARGED AT THE GHOST.

Ghost: *visibly panics* "Wait, what—"

Soo-ho: **TAGS THE GHOST.**

BEEP!

"YOU WIN."

The lights flickered back on.

Principal Loh's voice boomed overhead.

"CONGRATULATIONS, WINNERS! YOUR NEXT CLUE IS..."

A piece of paper dropped from the ceiling.

"YOUR FINAL CHALLENGE WILL HAPPEN... ON THE SCHOOL TRIP."

Ji-ae: "OH, COME ON—"

JianHao: *groaning* "Can we have one normal trip? Just one?"

Madeline: *grinning* "NEVER."

Destination: A Remote Island Resort.

Expectation: A peaceful getaway.
Reality: Absolute *chaos.*

Ji-ae: **"I feel like something *terrible* is going to happen."**

Soo-ho: **"You say that every time, and you're always right."**

Denise: *yawning* "Can we just sleep on the bus? I'm exhausted from that stupid ghost game."

JianHao: *grinning* "Nope. It's time for—"

Madeline: *interrupts* **"ROAD TRIP CHAOS."**

Ji-ae: *groaning* "I regret everything."

Each student was randomly assigned a **bus seat partner.**

Ji-ae: **"Please be Soo-ho. Please be Soo-ho."**

Announcement: *"Ji-ae, you're with—"*

DENISE.

Ji-ae: *horrified* "NOOOOO."

Denise: *grinning* "Oh, this is going to be FUN."

Meanwhile...

Soo-ho: "Who am I sitting with?"

Announcement:"*Soo-ho, you're with... MAD—*"

Ji-ae: "OH ABSOLUTELY NOT."

Teacher: "Ji-ae, you can't change seats."

Ji-ae: **"WATCH ME."**

Ji-ae ended up stuck with Denise, while Soo-ho sat with **Madeline** (who was *thrilled*).

Denise: *whispering* "Ji-ae, let's prank the entire bus."

Ji-ae: "Denise, no."

Denise: "Denise, YES."

One hour later...

JianHao: **"WHY IS THERE A FAKE SPIDER ON MY FACE?!"**

Debbie: *screaming* "WHO SWAPPED MY DRINK WITH SOY SAUCE?!"

Soo-ho: *glaring at Ji-ae* "You had something to do with this, didn't you?"

Ji-ae: *innocently sipping her juice* "I have *no idea* what you're talking about."

Denise: *whispering* "Mission: **Success.**"

The students stepped off the bus and onto the white sand beach.

Ji-ae: "Okay, this is actually kind of nice."

Soo-ho: *smirking* "See? No disasters yet."

Right then, someone screamed.

JianHao: **"MY LUGGAGE FELL IN THE OCEAN."**

Denise: *cackling* "Looks like *your* clothes are *washed up* now."

JianHao: "THIS ISN'T FUNNY—WAIT, WHO TOOK MY SPARE CLOTHES?!"

Madeline was already wearing his hoodie.

Madeline: *grinning* "Mine now."

That night, after a *semi-chaotic* dinner (where Ji-ae *may or may not* have started a food fight with Denise), Principal Loh gathered the students.

Principal Loh: **"Welcome to your FINAL CHALLENGE."**

The students groaned.

Ji-ae: *muttering* "I *knew* they wouldn't let us relax."

Principal Loh: **"Tomorrow, you will all participate in... A TREASURE HUNT."**

JianHao: **"OH, WE'RE GONNA DIE."**

Denise: *excited* "I hope there's a secret pirate curse."

Ji-ae: *grinning* "Actually... this could be fun."

Soo-ho: **"Or a total disaster."**

Ji-ae: **"Either way, it's going to be entertaining."**

The next morning, the students gathered at the beach, **half awake and already regretting their life choices.**

JianHao: *yawning* "Why are we doing this so early?"

Denise: *grinning* "Because *suffering builds character*."

Ji-ae: *groaning* "My character is already overdeveloped."

Principal Loh: **"Welcome to your FINAL CHALLENGE: The Ultimate Treasure Hunt."**

Madeline: "Oooh, are we gonna find real treasure?"

Principal Loh: *ignoring her* **"You will work in teams. The first group to find the treasure wins..."**

"A WEEK WITHOUT HOMEWORK."

The students: **"WHAAAAAT?!"**

Ji-ae: **"OH, WE'RE WINNING THIS."**

Soo-ho: *smirking* "That's the most motivated I've ever seen you."

Ji-ae: "Listen, I will **fight** for this."

Each student was placed into teams of **four.**

Ji-ae: **"PLEASE put me with Soo-ho."**

Teacher: *reading the teams*

- **Team 1:** JianHao, Debbie, Denise, Madeline
  - **Team 2:** Soo-ho, Ji-ae, Vincent, Tasha

Ji-ae: *cheering* "YESSSS!"

Denise: *mocking* "Aww, lovebirds together?"

Ji-ae: *deadpan* "Denise, I will throw you into the ocean."

Each team was given **a map with clues.**

First clue:
"Follow the footprints on the sand, to the cave where secrets stand."

Ji-ae: "Easy! Look for footprints."

Soo-ho: "But which ones? The beach is *covered* in footprints."

Tasha: "We could just... follow the other teams?"

Vincent: "No way! We need a **shortcut.**"

Ji-ae: "Ohhh, I like how you think."

And so, instead of walking, Ji-ae **grabbed a kayak.**

Soo-ho: *alarmed* "We are *not* kayaking across the beach."

Ji-ae: *already paddling* "Too late!"

Tasha: *cheering* "This is either genius or *very dangerous.*"

Vincent: *panicking* "I CAN'T SWIM."

Soo-ho: *sighing* "Why am I in this team?"

Meanwhile, JianHao's team was **losing their minds.**

Denise: **"WHO GAVE MAD ABOUT A MACHETE?!"**

Madeline: *grinning* "We're in the jungle! I need to be *prepared.*"

Debbie: **"PREPARED FOR WHAT?!"**

JianHao: **"JUST FOLLOW THE MAP."**

Denise: **"I CAN'T, SOMEONE SPILLED COCONUT WATER ON IT."**

JianHao: "**...We are *so* doomed.**"

Ji-ae's shortcut? *A terrible idea.*

The kayak drifted too far, and they **ended up on the wrong side of the island.**

Vincent: **"I KNEW THIS WOULD HAPPEN."**

Tasha: **"Okay, don't panic, let's check the map."**

Ji-ae: **"…The map is wet."**

Soo-ho: **"…You dropped the map in the ocean, didn't you?"**

Ji-ae: **"I AM UNDER A LOT OF STRESS RIGHT NOW."**

As Ji-ae's team **wandered through the jungle**, they **tripped a hidden wire.**

A **net launched into the air—AND TRAPPED THEM.**

Ji-ae: **"ARE YOU KIDDING ME?!"**

Soo-ho: *hanging upside down* "I *knew* something like this would happen."

Vincent: **"I BLAME JI-AE."**

Tasha: **"WELL, THIS IS EMBARRASSING."**

Ji-ae: **"OKAY, NOBODY PANIC."**

Soo-ho: **"Ji-ae, YOU'RE the one panicking. Your mouth says 'NOBODY PANIC' but your face says 'PANIC'."**

Ji-ae: **"I HAVE EVERY RIGHT TO PANIC."**

After being trapped **for too long**, Ji-ae's chest tightened.

Her breaths grew **shaky**. Her hands trembled. The world felt **smaller**.

Soo-ho: *immediately noticing* **"Ji-ae… breathe."**

Ji-ae: *tears forming* "I can't—I—I feel trapped—I can't—"

Soo-ho: *softly* "Hey, hey. Look at me."

Ji-ae's panicked eyes met his.

Soo-ho: **"You're not alone. I'm right here. Just breathe with me, okay?"**

He held her hands, squeezing them gently.

Inhale.

Exhale.

Slowly, Ji-ae's breathing steadied.

Soo-ho: **"That's it. You're okay."**

Ji-ae: *sniffling* "I hate this stupid net."

Tasha: "Okay, that was **really sweet,** but CAN SOMEONE GET US OUT?!"

Location: Suspended in a net. **Status:** Annoyed.

Ji-ae: **"Okay, I've had enough of this. How do we get down?"**

Vincent: **"I dunno... maybe SCREAM FOR HELP?!"**

Tasha: *deadpan* **"Yeah, let's alert wild animals too. Genius."**

Soo-ho: **"Let's stay calm. There has to be a way—"**

Ji-ae: *grinning* **"Oh, there's a way."**

She pulled out... A POCKET KNIFE.

Vincent: **"WHERE DID YOU GET THAT?!"**

Ji-ae: *innocently* "A magician never reveals her secrets."

Soo-ho: *eyeing her* "You stole it from Madeline, didn't you?"

Ji-ae: "Look, it's either this or we wait for rescue."

Soo-ho: *sighing* **"Just cut the ropes."**

Ji-ae carefully **cut the net.**

Tasha: **"Okay, SLOWLY—"**

SNAP!

BOOM.

They CRASHED into the ground.

Vincent: *groaning* "I hate this trip."

Tasha: *brushing off leaves* "I hate all of you."

Soo-ho: *rubbing his head* "That could've gone worse."

Ji-ae: *smugly* "But we survived. That's what matters."

Vincent: *sarcastic* "Wow, thanks for your *great leadership.*"

After escaping, they **found a mysterious note** under a tree.

"Turn left at the hollow oak, where rivals meet and alliances break."

Ji-ae: "Okay, this feels **suspicious.**"

Soo-ho: "Because it *is.*"

They followed the clue... and **found something shocking.**

JIANHAO'S TEAM... ALREADY DIGGING UP THE TREASURE.

Ji-ae: **"YOU TRAITORS."**

Denise: *grinning* "Oh, were we supposed to *wait* for you?"

JianHao: "Hey, first come, first serve!"

Madeline: *laughing* "Aww, you guys look so betrayed."

Tasha: **"THAT HOMEWORK PASS IS OURS."**

Ji-ae: *rolling up sleeves* **"WE FIGHT."**

While they fought...

The teachers arrived.

Principal Loh: *clearing throat* **"So... who actually has the treasure?"**

Silence.

Then—

Denise: "Uh, JianHao?"

JianHao: "I THOUGHT YOU HAD IT."

Madeline: "WAIT—WHERE DID IT GO?!"

Everyone looked around.

And then...

Debbie walked up with the treasure box.

Debbie: *smiling sweetly* **"I took it while you were all fighting. Thanks for the distraction."**

SHE. WALKED. AWAY. WITH. THE. PRIZE.

Ji-ae: **"...NO WAY."**

Denise: **"I CAN'T EVEN BE MAD."**

Soo-ho: *laughing* "That was the most legendary move I've ever seen."

Ji-ae: **"I NEED TO LEARN FROM HER."**

Debbie: **"Better luck next time, losers."**

As the sun set, the students sat by the bonfire, **bruised, tired, but laughing.**

Ji-ae: "Okay, I *kinda* admit... that was fun."

Soo-ho: *smirking* "Told you."

Ji-ae: *smiling* "Shut up."

And just like that... their chaotic school trip came to an end.

As the students returned, a **new problem arose.**

The **Titan Academy Gossip Page** posted:

"Secrets were revealed on the trip... who's hiding something? Stay tuned."

Ji-ae: **"Oh, COME ON. Who is behind this?!"**

Soo-ho: *serious* **"We're going to find out."**

Ji-ae: *"Alright, listen up. We have a mission."*

Soo-ho: *"A very important mission."*

Vincent: *"Are we sneaking into the teacher's lounge to steal exam papers?"*

Ji-ae: **"...No."**

Tasha: *"Are we switching out JianHao's shampoo with slime?"*

JianHao: **"WHAT?!"**

Ji-ae: *ignoring him* **"No, but we're writing that down for later."**

Soo-ho: **"We're investigating something *very* serious."**

Madeline: *"Oh? What?"*

Ji-ae: **"WHO LOCKED US UP DURING THE TRIP?!"**

Step 1: Gathering Evidence

Ji-ae and Soo-ho sat at their **makeshift detective desk** (a cafeteria table with a 'TOP SECRET' sign made of sticky notes).

Tasha: *arms crossed* **"Okay, suspects?"**

Vincent: *raising hand* **"JianHao."**

JianHao: **"BRO, WHY?!"**

Ji-ae: *narrowing eyes* **"Hmm... actually, he's kinda right."**

JianHao: **"WHAT?!"**

Denise: *laughing* **"Yeah, you *do* have a history of pranks."**

JianHao: *offended* **"But I was LOCKED UP TOO!"**

Ji-ae: *"Fine. You're off the hook... for now."*

Step 2: The Interrogations

Suspect 1: Debbie

Ji-ae: **"Debbie, be honest. Was it you?"**

Debbie: *eating a muffin* **"Why would I waste my time on something that doesn't get me free food?"**

Ji-ae: *"...Good point."*

Suspect 2: Madeline

Soo-ho: *serious* **"Maddy, did you do it?"**

Madeline: *dramatic gasp* **"ME?! HOW DARE YOU ACCUSE ME!"**

Ji-ae: *"Okay, okay—"*

Madeline: *"Wait... would this have been an iconic villain move?"*

Ji-ae: *"...Yeah?"*

Madeline: *"...Dang it, I should have done it."*

(Madeline is innocent, but lowkey disappointed she didn't think of it.)

Step 3: The Unexpected Clue

Tasha: *"Okay, so if it wasn't us... who was it?"*

Denise: *squinting* "Wait. Who *wasn't* locked up with us?"

Ji-ae: "OH MY GOSH."

Soo-ho: "WE'RE IDIOTS."

Everyone turned to look at... VINCENT.

Vincent: "HOLD UP—WHY ARE YOU LOOKING AT ME?!"

Ji-ae: "WERE YOU LOCKED UP?"

Vincent: *nervously sweating* "...No?"

Tasha: "OH. MY. GOSH."

JianHao: "TRAITOR."

Step 4: The Confession

Ji-ae: *slamming hands on table* **"VINCENT. CONFESS."**

Vincent: **"OKAY, OKAY! It wasn't me, BUT—"**

Tasha: **"BUT WHAT?!"**

Vincent: *groaning* **"I might have *accidentally* helped."**

Soo-ho: **"EXPLAIN."**

Vincent: **"I *may* have told a certain someone that you guys were heading towards the lake... and then suddenly, you all disappeared."**

Ji-ae: **"WHO DID YOU TELL?!"**

Vincent: *whispering* **"...Denise."**

SILENCE.

Denise: **"WAIT, WAIT—HOLD ON—"**

Ji-ae: **"DENISE. IT WAS YOU?!"**

Denise: *laughing nervously* **"Listen, LISTEN. It was a prank! I was going to let you out after 5 minutes!"**

JianHao: *betrayed* **"SO IT WAS YOUUUUU."**

Denise: *shrugging* **"Oops?"**

Step 5: Revenge

Ji-ae: *cracking knuckles* **"Denise. You have officially declared war."**

Denise: **"Oh no."**

Soo-ho: *smirking* **"Better watch your back."**

Tasha: **"Sleep with one eye open."**

Vincent: **"I can't believe I snitched. I've failed as a best friend."**

JianHao: *laughing* **"This is the best day of my life."**

Denise: **"...I regret everything."**

MISSION COMPLETE: JUSTICE SERVED.

(...but Denise *better* be careful, because Ji-ae & Co. are **PLANNING REVENGE.**)

Step 1: The Planning Stage

Ji-ae: *"Alright, team. Denise thinks she can prank us? HA. It's time we show her who's boss."*

Soo-ho: *smirking* **"We're about to make her regret EVERYTHING."**

JianHao: **"I LIVE for this."**

Tasha: *cracking knuckles* **"I've been waiting for this moment my whole life."**

Vincent: **"I still feel bad for snitching, so count me in."**

Madeline: **"I'm only here to make sure we go down in history."**

Ji-ae: *nodding* **"Good. Now... here's the plan."**

Ji-ae pulls out a **whiteboard covered in evil doodles,** listing out **THE THREE STAGES OF PAYBACK.**

1. **Phase One: The 'Oh No, My Stuff!' Prank**
2. **Phase Two: The 'Denise, Why Is Everyone Ignoring You?' Trap**
3. **Phase Three: The Grand Finale™ (Chaos Unleashed).**

Let. The. Pranking. Begin.

Phase One: The 'Oh No, My Stuff!' Prank

Location: The Hallway
Target: Denise
Objective: Make her think she's losing her mind.

Denise walks into class, **but her chair is gone.**

Denise: **"...What the—?"**

She goes to grab her textbook. **It's missing.**

Denise: *"...Huh?"*

She reaches for her bag. **POOF. It's gone.**

Denise: **"HELLO?! WHERE IS EVERYTHING?!"**

Cue Ji-ae and the gang watching from behind the lockers, cackling.

Soo-ho: **"It's working."**

JianHao: **"This is my favorite day ever."**

Madeline: *whispering* **"Phase Two, GO."**

Phase Two: The 'Denise, Why Is Everyone Ignoring You?' Trap

Denise: **"Tasha, have you seen my bag?"**

Tasha: **"...."***stares at the ceiling like Denise doesn't exist.*

Denise: **"Uh... Vincent?"**

Vincent: **"...."***casually walks away.*

Denise: **"HELLO?! WHY IS NO ONE TALKING TO ME?!"**

Ji-ae: *fake shocked* **"Wait... guys. Do you hear something?"**

Soo-ho: *dramatic gasp* **"A ghost?!"**

JianHao: **"OH MY GOSH, THE CLASSROOM IS HAUNTED."**

Denise: **"I WILL KILL ALL OF YOU."**

Phase Three: The Grand Finale™ *(CHAOS*

UNLEASHED.)

Denise storms to the **cafeteria**, fuming.

Denise: *"Y'ALL BETTER STOP—"*

SPLAT.

A **bucket of flour** falls on her head.

Denise: "...."

The **entire cafeteria** BURSTS INTO LAUGHTER.

JianHao: *wheezing* **"SHE LOOKS LIKE A WALKING DONUT."**

Ji-ae & Soo-ho: *high-fiving* **"MISSION ACCOMPLISHED."**

Denise: **"...I hate all of you."**

Vincent: *offering a napkin* **"No hard feelings?"**

Denise: **"...It's ON."**

TO BE CONTINUED...

DENISE WILL STRIKE BACK.

The war is FAR from over. **And Titan Academy is NOT ready for what's coming next.**

The next day, Ji-ae sat outside near the school garden, her arms resting on her knees. After all the **chaos, pranks, and nonstop drama,** she just needed a second to breathe.

Soo-ho found her immediately.

Soo-ho: *"Skipping class?"*

Ji-ae: *"Not skipping. Just... hiding."*

Soo-ho: *chuckles* "From Denise?"

Ji-ae: *sighs* "From everyone."

Soo-ho sat beside her, his **presence instantly calming her.** Ji-ae didn't even have to explain—he just *knew.*

Ji-ae: *"It's like... everything at Titan Academy is always so loud. And sometimes, I just want to be alone."*

Soo-ho: *gently* **"Then I'll sit here with you."**

Ji-ae looked at him, her heart doing a *weird little flip.* **How was he always like this?** So understanding. So steady.

For a while, they just sat there. **No words. No interruptions.** Just... them.

Until—

RUMBLE.

Ji-ae's stomach **betrayed her.**

Soo-ho: "**…Was that your stomach?**"

Ji-ae: *horrified* "**NO.**"

Soo-ho: *grinning* "**You sure? Because it sounds like it's crying for food.**"

Ji-ae: "**SHUT UP.**"

Soo-ho: "**Come on. I'll buy you something from the cafeteria.**"

Ji-ae: *muttering* "**This is so embarrassing.**"

Soo-ho just laughed and pulled her up by the wrist, **his touch lingering for just a second longer than necessary.**

In the cafeteria, Soo-ho placed a tray in front of Ji-ae.

Soo-ho: "**Eat. Before you pass out and blame me for it.**"

Ji-ae: "**Wow. So romantic.**"

Soo-ho: "**You want romance? Fine. I'll even cut your sandwich for you.**"*starts cutting it dramatically*

Ji-ae: *laughing* "**You're impossible.**"

As they ate, Ji-ae glanced around and noticed something. **People were staring. Whispering.**

Ji-ae: "**…Why is everyone looking at us?**"

Soo-ho: *shrugging* "**Maybe because we're sitting together?**"

Ji-ae: *suspicious* "**Or maybe because you just made me a sandwich like we're some kind of couple?**"

Soo-ho: *raising an eyebrow* "**Aren't we?**"

Ji-ae: "**….**"

Wait. WHAT.

ARE THEY?!

Her brain **froze.** Had they ever actually **defined** what they were? They spent **all their time together.** They had **moments.** They even **held hands in the rain.**

Ji-ae: *flustered* "**Are we…?**"

Soo-ho: "**Do you *want* us to be?**"

Ji-ae: "**….**"

HELLO?! WAS HE TRYING TO KILL HER?!

Her face was **on fire.** She had no idea how to answer.

But before she could, **Denise's loud voice cut through the cafeteria.**

Denise: "**ALRIGHT, YOU TWO. CONFESS. ARE YOU DATING OR WHAT?!**"

EVERYONE STARED.

Ji-ae: *panicked* **"I—We—"**

Soo-ho, the absolute menace, just SMIRKED.

Soo-ho: **"What do you think?"**

Denise: **"BRO, THAT'S NOT AN ANSWER."**

Ji-ae: **"I HATE ALL OF YOU."**

And just like that, **the entire school lost its mind.**

Ji-ae **practically ran** out of the cafeteria.

Ji-ae: *("What just happened?!")*

Soo-ho: **"Ji-ae, wait up!"**

But she **didn't wait.** She was **too flustered, too confused,** and needed a second to **breathe.**

Was Soo-ho serious? Was he just **teasing?** And why was her **heart racing so much?!**

Soo-ho found her on the school rooftop, **her usual hiding spot.**

Soo-ho: *gently* **"Are you mad?"**

Ji-ae: **"I just—WHAT WAS THAT?!"**

Soo-ho: **"What was what?"** *grinning*

Ji-ae: **"YOU KNOW WHAT."**

Soo-ho: **"...Oh, you mean when I basically implied we're together in front of the entire school?"**

Ji-ae: **"YES. THAT."**

Soo-ho: **"...Well?"**

Ji-ae: *flustered* **"WELL, WHAT?"**

Soo-ho: **"Are we?"**

Ji-ae: **"I—"***brain malfunctioning*

Soo-ho: **"Because, Ji-ae, if you're not sure, I can say it first."**

Ji-ae: **"...Say what?"**

Soo-ho: *softly, but completely serious* **"That I like you."**

BOOM.

Ji-ae.exe has stopped working.

Ji-ae: **"You—You do?!"**

Soo-ho: *laughing softly* **"You really didn't know?"**

Ji-ae: **"I—No?! How was I supposed to know?! You always tease me!"**

Soo-ho: *shrugging* **"That's how I flirt."**

Ji-ae: **"YOU NEED A NEW STRATEGY."**

Soo-ho: **"Alright, then. Let me try something new."**

And then—before Ji-ae could react—he took her hand.

Ji-ae's heart **practically exploded.**

Soo-ho: *gently squeezing her hand* **"I like you, Ji-ae. And I don't want to just 'imply' things in front of people. I want you to know it. Clearly."**

Ji-ae: **"..."**

Ji-ae: **"...I like you too, idiot."**

Soo-ho: **"...I knew it."**

Ji-ae: *gasps* **"EXCUSE ME?"**

Soo-ho: **"You always get flustered around me."**

Ji-ae: **"LIES."**

Soo-ho: *smirking* **"Oh really? Should I list the times—"**

Ji-ae: **"NOPE. STOP TALKING."**

Soo-ho: *laughing* **"Fine. But now that we both know..."**

He **intertwined their fingers. Ji-ae forgot how to breathe.**

Soo-ho: **"...What do you say we stop running from this?"**

Ji-ae: "...**Are you asking me out?**"

Soo-ho: "**I thought that was obvious.**"

Ji-ae: "**Well, you should say it properly!**"

Soo-ho: "**Alright. Ji-ae, will you—**"

CRASH.

The door **slammed open.**

Denise: "**I KNEW IT. I KNEW YOU TWO WERE HAVING A MOMENT.**"

JianHao: "**WE JUST WITNESSED HISTORY.**"

Madeline: "**SOO-HO, YOU REALLY LOCKED IT IN.**"

Ji-ae: "**I CAN NEVER HAVE A SINGLE ROMANTIC MOMENT IN PEACE.**"

Soo-ho: *laughing* "**It's fine. We have all the time in the world.**"

Ji-ae **hated how soft that made her feel.**

The Next Day at Titan Academy...

Ji-ae **regretted everything.**

Because the **moment** she stepped into school…

EVERYONE WAS STARING.

And whispering.

And giggling.

WHY?!

Denise ran up to her, **grinning like a lunatic.**

Denise: **"SOOOOO… HOW DOES IT FEEL TO BE THE MOST TALKED ABOUT COUPLE IN SCHOOL?!"**

Ji-ae: **"WE ARE NOT—"**

JianHao: **"Oh please. Everyone saw Soo-ho holding your hand."**

Debbie: **"AND YOU WERE SMILING."**

Madeline: **"AND BLUSHING."**

Ji-ae: **"STOP MAKING THINGS UP—"**

Denise: **"Girl. We literally saw it."**

Ji-ae: **"…"**

Ji-ae: **"I am moving to another country."**

Meanwhile, Soo-ho...

Soo-ho walked down the hallway, completely **unbothered.**

Random Student 1: **"Dude. You and Ji-ae?"**

Random Student 2: **"Bro, the way you confessed?!
LEGENDARY."**

Random Student 3: **"Teach me your ways."**

Soo-ho: *smirking* **"Just be yourself."**

Random Student 3: **"But I'm not as smooth as you."**

Soo-ho: **"Tragic."**

Ji-ae **stormed up to Soo-ho.**

Ji-ae: **"YOU. THIS IS YOUR FAULT."**

Soo-ho: *raising an eyebrow* **"What is?"**

Ji-ae: **"THE ENTIRE SCHOOL THINKS WE'RE
TOGETHER."**

Soo-ho: *grinning* **"Aren't we?"**

Ji-ae: **"...."**

Soo-ho: **"You said you liked me."**

Ji-ae: **"...."**

Soo-ho: **"So unless you changed your mind—"**

Ji-ae: **"I DIDN'T."** *pauses* **"...I mean, no, I didn't change my mind."**

Soo-ho: *softly* **"Good."**

Ji-ae's heart did that **annoying little flip again.**

Soo-ho: **"Then what's the problem?"**

Ji-ae: *muttering* **"I just... wasn't ready for everyone to know."**

Soo-ho: *chuckles* **"Too late now."**

Ji-ae **groaned.**

And then—

Denise (yelling): **"JUST KISS ALREADY!"**

The **entire hallway exploded** with laughter.

Ji-ae: **"I AM GOING TO THROW SOMETHING."**

Soo-ho: **"Go easy on them. They're just excited."**

Ji-ae: **"Excited for what?"**

Soo-ho: *grinning* **"Our love story."**

Ji-ae: **"I HATE YOU."**

Soo-ho: **"No, you don't."**

Ji-ae: "...**UGH.**"

Then there came a surprise.
A transfer student. Her name was Kim Hwa Young.

Kim Hwa Young stood in front of Titan Academy's massive gates, gripping the straps of her backpack tightly. *New school, new people, new start.* She took a deep breath and stepped in.

The moment she entered the classroom, everyone turned to stare.

"Oh? A new student?" Denise whispered to Debbie.

Hwa Young smiled nervously. "Hi, I'm Kim Hwa Young. I just transferred here."

"Welcome to Titan Academy, Hwa Young!" JianHao said dramatically. "Hope you survive."

"Don't scare her," Ji-ae scolded playfully, stepping forward. "Hi, I'm Kang Ji-ae. You can sit with me if you want."

Hwa Young smiled. "Thanks!"

As the day went on, Ji-ae and Hwa Young clicked instantly. They talked about K-dramas, music, and even Ji-ae's boyfriend, Lee Soo-ho.

"I swear, he acts all serious, but he's secretly soft," Ji-ae whispered, grinning.

"I can't believe you're dating Lee Soo-ho! He's literally perfect," Hwa Young gushed.

Ji-ae smirked. "You'll find someone too."

And she did. Faster than she expected.

During break, Hwa Young accidentally bumped into someone in the hallway. Books fell to the ground.

"Sorry! I wasn't—" She looked up and froze.

Han Seo-jun.

Titan Academy's bad boy, with his leather jacket, smirk, and that ridiculously good-looking face.

"No worries," Seo-jun said, helping her pick up her books. "New girl, right?"

Hwa Young nodded, feeling her face heat up. "Yeah… I'm Kim Hwa Young."

Seo-jun grinned. "Well, Hwa Young, better watch where you're going next time. Wouldn't want you crashing into someone worse."

Over the next few weeks, she somehow kept running into Seo-jun. In the hallways, in the cafeteria, even during after-school study sessions. He started teasing her. She started teasing him back.

"You're obsessed with me," she joked one day.

"Pfft, as if." But his smirk said otherwise.

Ji-ae noticed everything. "Oh my gosh. You guys have chemistry."

"Shut up!" Hwa Young groaned, but she couldn't stop smiling.

Then, one rainy afternoon, Seo-jun found her waiting outside the school gates, frowning at the storm.

"Forgot your umbrella?" he asked, twirling his own.

"Obviously," she sighed.

"Guess you'll have to walk home with me." He held out his umbrella, his ears turning pink.

Hwa Young's heart did a little flip.

And just like that, Kim Hwa Young and Han Seo-jun became a thing.

Ji-ae was overjoyed. "BESTIES AND DATING HOT GUYS? We're literally winning at life."

Hwa Young laughed, linking arms with Ji-ae as they walked to class. "Forever."

One day, Denise suddenly started,
Denise: **"So. When's the first date?"**

Ji-ae: *choking on her water* **"EXCUSE ME?"**

JianHao: **"You two are a thing now. Dates are mandatory."**

Debbie: **"It's basically in the relationship rulebook."**

Madeline: **"It's, like, illegal to date and NOT go on a date."**

Ji-ae: **"WHERE IS THIS RULEBOOK?!"**

Denise: **"Oh, we made it up just now."**

Soo-ho: *smirking* **"Sounds fair to me."**

Ji-ae: **"...Why are you like this?"**

Soo-ho: **"Because I like seeing you flustered."**

Ji-ae: **"I AM NOT FLUSTERED."** *definitely flustered*

Denise: **"SO IT'S SETTLED. YOU TWO ARE GOING ON A DATE."**

Ji-ae: **"Okay. We'll just do something simple. No big deal."**

Denise: **"Nope. It has to be romantic."**

JianHao: **"AND eventful."**

Debbie: **"AND unforgettable."**

Madeline: **"AND with a little bit of chaos."**

Ji-ae: **"WHY WOULD I WANT CHAOS?!"**

Denise: *grinning* **"You're dating Soo-ho. Chaos is included."**

Soo-ho: *nodding* **"She's not wrong."**

Ji-ae: **"...I need a refund."**

Soo-ho picked her up for their **"normal, no big deal"** date.

Everything was **fine** until...

1. They got on the bus, and **it broke down halfway.**
2. They decided to **walk to the restaurant**... and it **started raining.**
3. Ji-ae slipped on a **banana peel.**
4. Soo-ho **caught her... but also fell.**
5. A little kid pointed at them and yelled **"LOOK, THEY'RE IN LOVE!"**
6. An **old couple clapped.**
7. The waiter at the restaurant was **Denise's cousin.** Who **immediately took photos.**
8. Soo-ho's order got **mixed up, and he ate the spiciest thing on the menu.**
9. Ji-ae laughed **too hard and choked on her drink.**
10. They tried to **leave quietly... but knocked over a whole tray of drinks.**

Ji-ae: **"That was... the worst date in history."**

Soo-ho: **"Was it?"***grinning*

Ji-ae: **"…What are you smiling about?"**

Soo-ho: **"I had fun."**

Ji-ae: **"…ARE YOU OKAY?"**

Soo-ho: **"We had an adventure. That's what matters."**

Ji-ae: **"…You are so weird."**

Soo-ho: *shrugging* **"And yet, you still like me."**

Ji-ae: **"…"**

Ji-ae: **"…Shut up."**

Soo-ho: *laughing* **"Never."**

Ji-ae **barely** stepped into the school before—

Denise: **"TELL ME EVERYTHING."**

JianHao: **"Did he kiss you?"**

Debbie: **"Did you hold hands?"**

Madeline: **"Did he confess his eternal love?"**

Ji-ae: **"…CAN I BREATHE?!"**

Denise: **"No. Now SPILL."**

Ji-ae sighed, **defeated.**

Ji-ae: "**The bus broke down. It rained. I slipped. He fell. A kid screamed. Old people clapped. A waiter took photos. Soo-ho almost DIED from spicy food. I almost DIED from choking. We knocked over drinks. And now I'm never leaving my house again.**"

Denise: "**...ICONIC.**"

JianHao: "**A literal rom-com.**"

Debbie: "**I love this for you.**"

Madeline: "**Did you say 'I love you' at the end?**"

Ji-ae: "**NO!**"

Denise: "**Did he say it?**"

Ji-ae: "**NO.**"

JianHao: *smirking* "**Yet.**"

Ji-ae: "**I hate you all.**"

Soo-ho **knew** something was up the moment he walked into class.

Because **everyone** kept staring.

And whispering.

And... giggling??

Soo-ho: "...**What did you do?**"

Denise: *grinning* "**Oh nothing~**"

JianHao: *grinning* "**Just, you know, spread the good word.**"

Debbie: "**Of your beautifully tragic, hilarious date.**"

Soo-ho: "...**You guys are the worst.**"

Madeline: "**No. We're your biggest fans.**"

Soo-ho: "...**I am never dating in public again.**"

Denise: "**Too late. You're famous now.**"

Right when Ji-ae thought the chaos was **over**—

Principal: "**Attention, students! This year's school trip is officially happening! We're going to—**"

"**MYSTIC SPRINGS RESORT!**"

The **entire school screamed.**

Denise: "**OH. MY. GOSH. A BEACH TRIP?!**"

JianHao: "**AND HOT SPRINGS?!**"

Debbie: "**AND LUXURY ROOMS?!**"

Madeline: "**AND A FIVE-STAR BUFFET?!**"

Ji-ae: "...**Wait. This sounds... TOO good.**"

Denise: "**What do you mean?**"

Ji-ae: "**Think about it. When has a school trip EVER gone smoothly?**"

Everyone **paused.**

Denise: "**...Never.**"

JianHao: "**...Literally never.**"

Debbie: "**...We always end up in disaster.**"

Madeline: "**...So what's gonna happen this time?**"

Ji-ae: "**I don't know.**"

Soo-ho: *grinning* "**But whatever it is... we're ready.**"

The moment the students boarded the **bus**, the chaos **officially began.**

Denise: "**OKAY, WHO BROUGHT SNACKS?!**"

JianHao: *pulling out an entire bag* "**I GOT YOU.**"

Debbie: *glaring* "**DID YOU BRING FOR EVERYONE?**"

JianHao: "**...No?**"

Cue a riot.

Meanwhile, Ji-ae and Soo-ho were trying to **survive** in their seats.

Ji-ae: *whispering* "**Why do I feel like this is going to be a disaster?**"

Soo-ho: *grinning* "**Because it always is.**"

Denise: "**GUYS, LET'S PLAY 'TRUTH OR DARE'!**"

Ji-ae: "**NO.**"

Denise: "**YES.**"

JianHao: "**JI-AE, TRUTH OR DARE?**"

Ji-ae: "**I SAID NO—**"

Denise: "**DARE.**"

Ji-ae: "**I— WAIT WHAT? YOU CAN'T CHOOSE FOR ME—**"

JianHao: *grinning* "**I dare you... to sit on Soo-ho's lap for five minutes.**"

The **entire bus** screamed.

Ji-ae: "**EXCUSE ME?!**"

Denise: "**I LOVE THIS.**"

Debbie: "**THIS IS HISTORY.**"

Madeline: "**THIS IS CINEMA.**"

Soo-ho: *smirking* "**Well, rules are rules.**"

Ji-ae: **"I HATE ALL OF YOU."**

They finally arrived at **Mystic Springs Resort.**

The place was **huge.**

Ji-ae: **"Okay... maybe this won't be so bad."**

Denise: *gasping* **"LOOK AT THE POOL."**

JianHao: **"LOOK AT THE HOT SPRINGS."**

Debbie: **"LOOK AT THE BUFFET."**

Madeline: **"LOOK AT THE COUPLES' ACTIVITIES—"**

Ji-ae: **"NO."**

Soo-ho: *grinning* **"Yes."**

Ji-ae: **"Soo-ho, I swear—"**

Denise: **"OKAY, LET'S GO CHECK OUT OUR ROOMS."**

Denise: **"Okay, let's see who's rooming with who..."**

Ji-ae: **"Oh, I already know I'm with—"**

Denise: **"Soo-ho."**

Ji-ae: **"...EXCUSE ME?!"**

JianHao: *grinning* **"Yeah, the teachers assigned rooms. Sorry~"**

Debbie: **"HAVE FUN."**

Ji-ae: **"I REFUSE—"**

Soo-ho: *already dragging her away* **"C'mon, let's check out the room."**

Ji-ae: **"I HATE THIS SCHOOL."**

Ji-ae **stared** at the room.

One room.
One bed.
One Soo-ho.

Ji-ae: **"...There's only one bed."**

Soo-ho: **"Yep."**

Ji-ae: **"I'll sleep on the floor."**

Soo-ho: **"No, you won't."**

Ji-ae: **"Yes, I will."**

Soo-ho: **"No, you won't."**

Ji-ae: **"YES, I WILL—"**

Soo-ho: *grinning* **"Fine, I'll sleep on the floor with you."**

Ji-ae: **"...Wait, what?"**

Soo-ho: *shrugging* **"Not letting you suffer alone."**

Ji-ae: "...**Okay, now I feel bad.**"

Soo-ho: "**So just take the bed?**"

Ji-ae: "**No.**"

Soo-ho: "**Then we both suffer.**"

Ji-ae: "...**You are so annoying.**"

Soo-ho: "**And yet, you like me.**"

Ji-ae: "...**I need to go outside.**"

The Night Walk

The resort was **quiet** at night.
The air was **cool**, the stars **bright**, and the ocean **calm.**

Ji-ae stood by the shore, toes sinking into the cold sand.

Soo-ho: *walking up beside her* "**Couldn't sleep?**"

Ji-ae: *softly* "**Too much on my mind.**"

Soo-ho: "**Like what?**"

Ji-ae: "...**Everything.**"

Soo-ho: *watching her* "**You always overthink.**"

Ji-ae: "**And you never think.**"

Soo-ho: **"That's why we balance each other out."**

Ji-ae: *smirking* **"That was so cheesy."**

Soo-ho: **"And yet, you're smiling."**

Ji-ae **looked away.**

Soo-ho: **"Come here."**

Before she could react, he pulled her into a **hug.**

A warm, soft, **perfect** hug.

Ji-ae: **"…What are you doing?"**

Soo-ho: **"Shutting your brain off for a second."**

Ji-ae **froze.**

His arms were **warm.**
His scent was **calming.**
Her heart was **racing.**

Soo-ho: *softly* **"Just… stop thinking, Ji-ae."**

And for the first time in a long time, she did.

Ji-ae didn't know how long they stood there, just **holding each other.**

The ocean waves crashed softly in the background, the stars twinkled overhead, but all she could **feel** was Soo-ho.

His arms around her.
His warmth.
His heartbeat.

It was **dangerous.**

Because it felt **too good.**

Ji-ae: *softly* "**...You can let go now.**"

Soo-ho: *low voice* "**Do you want me to?**"

Ji-ae **froze.**

Her **mind** screamed yes.
Her **heart** whispered no.

Ji-ae: "**...I don't know.**"

Soo-ho: *smirking* "**Honest answer.**"

His voice was **deep**, his eyes **dark**, and something about the way he looked at her made her **heart race.**

Ji-ae: *muttering* "**You're annoying.**"

Soo-ho: *grinning* "**And yet, you're still here.**"

Ji-ae **scowled.** "**I'm leaving.**"

She turned—
But Soo-ho caught her wrist.

Ji-ae: *heart skipping* "**Soo-ho—**"

Soo-ho: *softly* **"Don't run."**

Ji-ae **stopped.**

Soo-ho: **"You always do that."**

Ji-ae: **"Do what?"**

Soo-ho: **"Run when things get real."**

Ji-ae: **"That's not true."**

Soo-ho: *watching her* **"Then why are you avoiding this?"**

Ji-ae **stared at him.**

Because it was **too much.**
Because it made her feel **too much.**

And yet—

Ji-ae: *quietly* **"...I don't know what to do with you."**

Soo-ho: *grinning* **"You could kiss me."**

Ji-ae: **"EXCUSE ME?!"**

Soo-ho: **"Just saying."**

Ji-ae: **"I HATE YOU."**

She **shoved** him and stormed back toward the resort.

But she didn't see his **knowing smirk** as he watched her
go.

Because **this time,** she wasn't running.

Ji-ae **stormed** back into their room, her heart **still racing.**

Why did Soo-ho have to be like that?
Why did he always have to **tease her** like that?
Why did he—

Soo-ho: *walking in behind her* **"You left in a hurry."**

Ji-ae: **"Shut up."**

Soo-ho: **"You're flustered."**

Ji-ae: **"I AM NOT—"**

Soo-ho: **"Look at you, all worked up over one little
comment."**

Ji-ae turned around, **ready to fight—**

But **froze.**

Soo-ho had **taken off his hoodie**, leaving him in just his
black T-shirt, his hair slightly messy from the ocean
breeze.

And **oh no.**

Why did he have to look **that good?**

Ji-ae: *clearing her throat* "**You're annoying.**"

Soo-ho: *smirking* "**You already said that.**"

Ji-ae: *grumbling* "**Because it's true.**"

Soo-ho: "**And yet, you can't stop looking at me.**"

Ji-ae: "**I CAN'T—**"

Soo-ho stepped closer. **Too close.**

Ji-ae **backed up.**

Her **legs hit the bed.**

Soo-ho: *softly* "**Are you gonna run again?**"

Ji-ae: *narrowing her eyes* "**You're doing this on purpose.**"

Soo-ho: "**Maybe.**"

Ji-ae: "**Why?**"

Soo-ho: *low voice* "**Because you look cute when you're flustered.**"

Ji-ae: "**...I hate you.**"

Soo-ho: *grinning* "**You keep saying that.**"

Ji-ae: "**Because it's TRUE.**"

Soo-ho: *leaning in slightly* "**Then why are you blushing?**"

Ji-ae: **"I'M NOT—"**

Soo-ho **laughed.A deep, warm, teasing laugh.**

Ji-ae **grabbed a pillow and threw it at his face.**

Soo-ho: **"AH—"**

Ji-ae: **"SLEEP ON THE FLOOR."**

Soo-ho: *grinning* **"Only if you join me."**

Ji-ae **let out a frustrated scream and dove under the covers, refusing to look at him.**

Her heart was **still pounding.**
Her face was **still warm.**
And Soo-ho's voice **still echoed in her mind.**

"Because you look cute when you're flustered."

She was doomed.

Ji-ae **tried** to sleep.

She really did.

But how could she, when **Soo-ho was right there?**

On the floor, just inches away, his breathing **steady** in the quiet night.

Ji-ae: **"...Are you asleep?"**

Soo-ho: **"…Nope."**

Ji-ae: *softly* **"Why not?"**

Soo-ho: *smirking* **"Because someone threw a pillow at my face and told me to sleep on the floor."**

Ji-ae: *rolling her eyes* **"You deserved it."**

Soo-ho: *chuckling* **"Did I?"**

Ji-ae: *muttering* **"Yes."**

Silence.

Soft.
Warm.
Comfortable.

And then—

Soo-ho: *gently* **"Come down here."**

Ji-ae: *freezing* **"…What?"**

Soo-ho: *quietly* **"It's cold."**

Ji-ae **knew** it was an excuse.

And yet—

Before she could overthink, she **grabbed her pillow** and slipped onto the floor beside him.

Soo-ho: *softly* "**...I didn't think you'd actually do it.**"

Ji-ae: "**Shut up.**"

Soo-ho **grinned.**

Their shoulders **touched.**

Ji-ae: *whispering* "**Soo-ho?**"

Soo-ho: "**Mm?**"

Ji-ae: "**...Do you think things would be different if we weren't always arguing?**"

Soo-ho: "**...Maybe.**"

Ji-ae: "**Would it be... better?**"

Soo-ho: *softly* "**I don't think so.**"

Ji-ae turned to face him, their noses **almost brushing.**

Ji-ae: *barely above a whisper* "**Why not?**"

Soo-ho: *watching her* "**Because then I wouldn't get to see this side of you.**"

Ji-ae: "**...What side?**"

Soo-ho: "**The one that stays. The one that doesn't run.**"

Ji-ae's breath **caught.**

He was **too close.**
The air was **too warm.**
And the look in his eyes was **too much.**

Ji-ae: "**…Soo-ho.**"

Soo-ho: *softly* "**Yeah?**"

Ji-ae: "**I hate you.**"

Soo-ho **laughed.**

And this time—
Ji-ae didn't pull away.

Soo-ho's laugh faded into a **gentle silence.**

Ji-ae could still feel it, though.
The warmth of it.
The way it **wrapped around her** like a feeling she wasn't
ready to name.

Ji-ae: *softly* "**…Why do you always do that?**"

Soo-ho: "**Do what?**"

Ji-ae: "**Laugh when I say I hate you.**"

Soo-ho: *grinning* "**Because I know you don't mean it.**"

Ji-ae **huffed**, turning her head away—
But Soo-ho **reached out**, gently tucking a strand of her
hair behind her ear.

Ji-ae: *heart skipping* "…What are you doing?"

Soo-ho: *softly* "**Looking at you.**"

Ji-ae **swallowed.**

Soo-ho: *whispering* "**You're prettier when you're not mad at me.**"

Ji-ae: "**…I'm always mad at you.**"

Soo-ho: *grinning* "**And yet, here you are. Lying next to me.**"

Ji-ae: "**…Shut up.**"

But she didn't move.

And neither did he.

The silence between them wasn't **awkward.**
It was **full.**

Of unspoken things.
Of almost-moments.
Of something **dangerously close to falling.**

Ji-ae: *whispering* "**…Goodnight, Soo-ho.**"

Soo-ho: "**Goodnight, Ji-ae.**"

And just before she drifted off, she swore she felt him **brush his fingers against hers.**

Ji-ae **regretted everything.**

It was **early.**
She was **tired.**
And their class had been assigned a **hiking trip.**

Madeline: **"Why are we even doing this?"**

Denise: **"Team-building."**

Debbie: **"You mean suffering."**

Ji-ae groaned, pulling her hoodie over her head. **She was NOT built for this.**

Soo-ho: **"What's wrong?"**

Ji-ae: **"I don't want to be here."**

Soo-ho: **"I thought you liked challenges."**

Ji-ae: **"I like challenges where I don't have to climb a mountain before breakfast."**

Soo-ho: *laughing* **"I'll carry you if you pass out."**

Ji-ae: **"I WILL NEVER LET YOU CARRY ME."**

Soo-ho: *grinning* **"We'll see."**

JianHao clapped his hands together, standing at the front. **"Alright, everyone! Let's get moving before the sun gets too hot."**

Ji-ae **groaned.**

And so, the disaster **began.**

Fifteen minutes into the hike—
Ji-ae was **already suffering.**

Ji-ae: *panting* **"This... is... actual... torture..."**

Denise: *gasping for breath* **"I thought we were... students... not mountain climbers!"**

Madeline: **"I'd rather be in detention."**

Debbie: **"Same."**

Meanwhile—Soo-ho was **walking like it was a casual stroll.**

Soo-ho: *grinning* **"You guys are so weak."**

Ji-ae shot him a **death glare.**

Ji-ae: *gasping* **"Shut... up... Soo-ho."**

Soo-ho: *teasing* **"Need help?"**

Ji-ae: **"I'd rather roll off this mountain than let you help me."**

Soo-ho: *laughing* **"Noted."**

JianHao, walking ahead, turned around. **"Come on, guys! We're almost at the first checkpoint!"**

Ji-ae: *dramatic* "**I won't make it.**"

Soo-ho: "**Yes, you will.**"

Ji-ae: "**No, I won't.**"

Soo-ho: "**Ji-ae.**"

Ji-ae: *whining* "**Soo-ho.**"

Soo-ho: *sighing* "**Fine.**"

Before Ji-ae could react—
Soo-ho **grabbed her hand.**

Ji-ae: "**WHAT ARE YOU—**"

Soo-ho: "**Helping you.**"

Ji-ae: *shocked* "**Let go!**"

Soo-ho: *grinning* "**No.**"

Ji-ae: "**I—**"

And then—
He **pulled her forward.**

Ji-ae **stumbled**, her fingers **tangling with his.**

Ji-ae: *flustered* "**You—YOU CAN'T JUST HOLD MY HAND LIKE THIS!**"

Soo-ho: *smirking* "**Why not?**"

Ji-ae: **"Because—BECAUSE—"**

Denise: **"Oooohhhh."** ?

Madeline: **"You guys are holding hands?"**

Debbie: **"Ji-ae, are you blushing?"**

Ji-ae: **"I AM NOT."**

Soo-ho: *innocent* **"Then why aren't you letting go?"**

Ji-ae: *realizing* **"...WHAT."**

She **yanked her hand away**, face burning. **She hated him. So much.**

Soo-ho just **grinned.**

And continued walking—**like he didn't just ruin her entire day.**

After another **torturous** ten minutes—
Ji-ae **wanted to cry.**

Ji-ae: **"This hike is never-ending."**

Denise: **"Are we actually going up or are we just walking in circles?"**

Madeline: **"At this point, I don't care. I'm lying down the moment we stop."**

Debbie: **"Same."**

Meanwhile—
Soo-ho was still **walking like a hiking pro.**

Soo-ho: **"I don't get why you guys are struggling."**

Ji-ae: **"I don't get why you're still talking."**

Soo-ho: *grinning* **"Want me to carry you?"**

Ji-ae: **"I'D RATHER DIE."**

Soo-ho: *laughing* **"Noted."**

JianHao, standing up ahead, turned around. **"Alright, break time! We'll rest here for a bit."**

Ji-ae: **"Finally."**

She **immediately sat down** on a rock, sighing in relief. Soo-ho **sat next to her.**

Ji-ae: *suspicious* **"...Why are you sitting here?"**

Soo-ho: *smirking* **"Because I like watching you suffer."**

Ji-ae: **"...I hate you."**

Soo-ho: *grinning* **"I know."**

The break **ended too soon,** and they continued hiking.

Ji-ae was **exhausted.**

Her legs felt like **jelly.**
Her feet **hurt.**
And the path was getting **steeper.**

Ji-ae: **"I can't do this."**

Soo-ho: *teasing* **"Don't be dramatic."**

Ji-ae: **"I'M NOT DRAMA—AHHHH!"**

One second—**she was walking.**
The next—**she stepped on a loose rock and slipped.**

Ji-ae: **"OH MY—"**

Before she could fall—
Soo-ho **reacted instantly.**

He grabbed her wrist—pulled her towards him—and—

THUMP.

Ji-ae: **"…Ow."**

She landed **straight on Soo-ho.**

Soo-ho: *groaning* **"…You okay?"**

Ji-ae: **"…WHY AM I ON TOP OF YOU?!"**

Soo-ho: *grinning* **"Because you fell for me."**

Ji-ae: **"…I'M GOING TO PUNCH YOU."**

Denise: *gasping* **"Oh my gosh, are you guys okay?!"**

Madeline: *smirking* **"Wait… is Ji-ae lying on Soo-ho?"**

Debbie: *laughing* **"That's… kinda romantic."**

Ji-ae: **"IT IS NOT."**

She **tried to get up—**
But Soo-ho's **hand was still on her waist.**

Ji-ae: **"…Soo-ho."**

Soo-ho: *smirking* **"Yeah?"**

Ji-ae: **"…Let go."**

Soo-ho: **"Say please."**

Ji-ae: **"…I'M GOING TO THROW YOU OFF THIS MOUNTAIN."**

Soo-ho: *grinning* **"You already threw yourself on me."**

Ji-ae: *face burning* **"I HATE YOU."**

Soo-ho just **laughed.**

And Ji-ae **hated how good it sounded.**

After **the most embarrassing fall of her life**, Ji-ae **refused** to look at Soo-ho.

Ji-ae: *grumbling* **"This is all your fault."**

Soo-ho: *grinning* "**How?**"

Ji-ae: "**You distracted me.**"

Soo-ho: *smirking* "**By being handsome?**"

Ji-ae: *DEADPAN* "**...I'm going to push you off the trail.**"

Denise: *laughing* "**Wow, Ji-ae, you're so flustered!**"

Madeline: *teasing* "**Yeah... you totally 'fell' for him.**"

Ji-ae: "**STOP.**"

Meanwhile, Soo-ho just **walked beside her like nothing happened.**

Which made Ji-ae even **angrier.**

She was **tired.**
She was **hungry.**
And she **swore this hike was never-ending.**

And then—

It happened.

One moment, Ji-ae was **walking with the group.**

The next—**they were gone.**

Ji-ae: "**...Where is everyone?**"

She turned around—
And realized she was **alone.**

Ji-ae: *panicking* "**…Oh no. Oh no no no no—**"

Leaves rustled behind her.

Ji-ae: *frozen* "**…Oh my god.**"

She **slowly turned around.**

And there was—

Soo-ho.

Ji-ae: "**…WHY ARE YOU HERE?!**"

Soo-ho: "**…Why are YOU here?**"

Ji-ae: "**I don't know! I was walking, and then—EVERYONE DISAPPEARED.**"

Soo-ho: "**…You got lost.**"

Ji-ae: "**No, I—**"

Soo-ho: *raising an eyebrow*

Ji-ae: "**…Fine. Maybe.**"

Soo-ho: *sighing* "**Come on. Let's find the others.**"

Ji-ae: *grumbling* "**This is all YOUR fault.**"

Soo-ho: **"How? I wasn't even near you when you got lost."**

Ji-ae: **"…Shut up."**

Soo-ho: *grinning* **"You're unbelievable."**

Ji-ae: **"And you're annoying."**

Soo-ho: **"Yet here we are. Alone. In the woods. Together."**

Ji-ae: **"Oh my god, stop making this sound romantic."**

Soo-ho: *smirking* **"Who said I was?"**

Ji-ae: *fuming* **"I SWEAR—"**

But before she could yell at him—

A loud noise came from the trees.

Ji-ae: **"…What was that?"**

Soo-ho: **"…Not sure."**

Ji-ae: *whispering* **"It's probably a bear."**

Soo-ho: **"There are no bears here."**

Ji-ae: **"You don't know that!"**

Soo-ho: **"It's probably just a bird."**

Ji-ae: *whispering* **"A DEMONIC bird."**

Soo-ho: *sighing* **"Come on, let's keep moving."**

Ji-ae: **"...You go first."**

Soo-ho: *smirking* **"Scared?"**

Ji-ae: *deadpan* **"No. I just think if something attacks, it should get you first."**

Soo-ho: **"...Wow."**

Ji-ae: **"You deserve it."**

Soo-ho just **laughed.**

And Ji-ae **hated** how **it made her heart skip.**

Ji-ae: **"Okay, we've been walking forever. Are we even going the right way?"**

Soo-ho: *calmly* **"I think so."**

Ji-ae: **"YOU THINK?!"**

Soo-ho: **"Relax. We'll find them."**

Ji-ae: **"Relax?! We're literally LOST. In the middle of the WOODS. Where serial killers exist."**

Soo-ho: **"...Why do you know so much about serial killers?"**

Ji-ae: **"Because I watch documentaries."**

Soo-ho: *smirking* "**Of course you do.**"

Ji-ae: "**Shut up and focus on getting us out of here.**"

Soo-ho just **shook his head, grinning.**

As if things couldn't get worse—

A drop of rain fell.

Then another.

And within **seconds—**

BOOM.

Thunder.

Ji-ae: "**...Oh. My. God.**"

Soo-ho: "**We need to find shelter.**"

Ji-ae: "**NO KIDDING.**"

The rain poured harder.

They **ran** until they found a **small cave.**

Ji-ae: *panting* "**...We're going to die.**"

Soo-ho: *calmly* "**We're not going to die.**"

Ji-ae: "**We're lost, soaked, and trapped in a CAVE. What part of that is NOT leading to death?!**"

Soo-ho: *chuckling* **"You're dramatic."**

Ji-ae: **"And you're TOO CALM."**

Soo-ho just **shook his head.**

Ji-ae **shivered.**

The rain had completely **soaked her.**

Ji-ae: **"It's so cold."**

Soo-ho: **"...Come here."**

Ji-ae: **"What?!"**

Soo-ho: *rolling his eyes* **"You're shivering. Body heat helps."**

Ji-ae: **"...Are you seriously suggesting I cuddle with you?"**

Soo-ho: *smirking* **"I didn't say cuddle."**

Ji-ae: **"It SOUNDS like cuddling."**

Soo-ho: **"It's survival."**

Ji-ae: **"Survival my—"**

THUNDER CRASHED.

Ji-ae: *panicking* **"OKAY OKAY MOVE OVER."**

Soo-ho **opened his arms, and Ji-ae hesitantly moved closer.**

Ji-ae: *grumbling* **"If you tell anyone about this, I'll kill you."**

Soo-ho: *grinning* **"Your secret's safe with me."**

Ji-ae: **"...You're enjoying this, aren't you?"**

Soo-ho: *whispering* **"Maybe."**

Ji-ae: **"I hate you."**

Soo-ho: **"Sure you do."**

And yet—
Ji-ae didn't **pull away.**

The sound of **rain hitting the cave** filled the silence. Ji-ae **stared at the darkness ahead** while Soo-ho sat beside her, his warmth keeping her from freezing.

But her mind wasn't here anymore.

Her heart **pounded.**
Her breathing **quickened.**
Her chest felt **tight.**

She **couldn't breathe.**

The cave felt **smaller.**
The air felt **thicker.**

The shadows on the walls **twisted into old nightmares.**

And suddenly, she was **seven years old again.**

Ji-ae had gone on a **hike with her parents.** She had **run ahead**, chasing a butterfly, giggling—until she **lost the trail.**

It had been **funny at first.**

Until she realized **she was alone.**

She had wandered until she found a **small cave** and sat inside, waiting for her parents.

Then—**a landslide.**

The entrance had **collapsed.**

And Ji-ae had been **trapped.**

No light. No air.
Just **darkness.**

She had **screamed for help** until her voice **went hoarse.**

She had cried, gasping for air, trapped for what felt like **forever.**

By the time her parents **dug her out**, she had been **shaking, sobbing, unable to breathe.**

She never went on **hikes again.**

The **cave walls blurred.**
Her hands **shook.**
The memory **choked her.**

Ji-ae: "**...No, no, no...**"

Soo-ho: "**Ji-ae?**"

She **didn't respond.**

Soo-ho: "**Hey. What's wrong?**"

Then he saw her **trembling.**

Her **wide eyes staring at nothing.**

And he knew.

She was **having a panic attack.**

Soo-ho: "**Ji-ae, look at me.**"

She **couldn't.**

Soo-ho: "**Ji-ae.**"

Still **no response.**

So he did the only thing he could—

He **gently cupped her face.**

Soo-ho: "**Breathe with me.**"

She **gasped.**

Soo-ho: **"In."** *He inhaled slowly.*

Ji-ae tried, but her breath **hitched.**

Soo-ho: **"Again. In."**

She forced herself to **follow.**

Soo-ho: **"Now out."**

He exhaled. She **tried.**

Her chest **shook,** but she **kept going.**

Soo-ho: **"That's it. Just focus on me."**

Ji-ae **blinked.**

The cave was **still there.**
The shadows were **still dark.**

But now, there was also **Soo-ho.**

Warm.
Calm.
Safe.

Her breathing **slowed.**

She **leaned into his touch.**

Soo-ho **stroked her cheek.**

Soo-ho: *softly* **"You're okay."**

Ji-ae: **"...I hate caves."**

Soo-ho: *chuckling* **"I figured."**

After a while, the thunder **faded.**

The sky turned a soft **gray.**

Ji-ae: *mumbling* **"...We should find the others."**

Soo-ho: **"Are you okay to walk?"**

Ji-ae: *nodding* **"Yeah."**

Soo-ho **stood up first, then offered his hand.**

Ji-ae hesitated... then **took it.**

As they walked, Soo-ho finally asked—

Soo-ho: **"Why do you get panic attacks?"**

Ji-ae: **"...It's stupid."**

Soo-ho: **"It's not."**

She sighed.

And then, for the first time, she **told someone.**

Told **him.**

And as she spoke, Soo-ho **never looked away.**

Never judged.
Never laughed.

Just **listened.**

And Ji-ae **felt lighter.**

Like maybe, just maybe—

She wasn't **trapped anymore.**

Ji-ae and Soo-ho **finally made it out of the cave**, stepping into the cool, damp forest. The rain had slowed to a drizzle, but the ground was still **muddy and slippery.**

Ji-ae: **"Great. Now where is everyone?"**

Soo-ho: **"They were supposed to be at the rest stop near the waterfall..."**

Ji-ae: **"So let's go."**

Soo-ho grabbed her wrist **before she could start walking.**

Soo-ho: **"Careful. The ground is still wet."**

Ji-ae: **"I can handle a little mud—"***slips immediately*

Soo-ho: **"Uh-huh."**

Before she could **fall face-first**, Soo-ho **caught her.**

Ji-ae blinked up at him.

Ji-ae: "…**You planned this.**"

Soo-ho smirked. **"You're just predictable."**

Ji-ae: **"Shut up."**

She straightened up, brushing herself off. But before she could move again, a **distant scream** echoed through the forest—

"AAAAHHH—OHMYGOD, THEY'RE ALIVE!!"

Through the trees, **Denise, Debbie, Madeline, and JianHao came RUNNING toward them.**

Denise: **"WHERE WERE YOU TWO?!"**

Debbie: **"WE THOUGHT YOU DIED!"**

JianHao: **"I WAS READY TO LEAD A RESCUE MISSION."**

Madeline: **"I WAS PREPARING A FUNERAL SPEECH."**

Ji-ae: **"…Excuse me?!"**

Denise: **"You disappeared! Then the storm hit! Then Soo-ho wasn't answering his phone! Then Ji-ae wasn't answering her phone! We thought—"**

Debbie: *dramatic gasp* **"—YOU ELOPED."**

Ji-ae: **"WHAT?!"**

JianHao: "...Wait, they didn't?"

Ji-ae: **"NO!"**

Soo-ho: *calmly* **"Not yet."**

Ji-ae: **"LEE SOO-HO."**

The group **exploded into chaos.**

Denise: **"WHERE WERE YOU?!"**

Ji-ae sighed. **"We got lost. Then we found a cave. Then we got stuck there because of the storm."**

Madeline: **"You spent the night... in a cave... alone... together...?"**

Ji-ae: **"Yes, and?"**

Debbie: **"OMG, THAT'S SO ROMANTIC."**

JianHao: *suspiciously* **"Wait. Why is Soo-ho looking at Ji-ae like that?"**

Ji-ae: **"Like what?"**

Denise: **"LIKE SHE'S HIS WHOLE WORLD."**

Ji-ae **whipped her head around.**

Soo-ho just **smirked.**

Ji-ae: **"...I hate all of you."**

The group **started heading back**, but Ji-ae noticed
something... different.

Soo-ho was **closer than usual.**

Normally, he walked a few steps ahead, but now—**he
stayed beside her.**

Every time she stumbled, he caught her.

Every time the path got tricky, he guided her.

Even when she told him **she was fine**, he still **hovered.**

Ji-ae: *whispering* **"Why are you being so... protective?"**

Soo-ho: *glancing at her* **"Do you not want me to be?"**

Ji-ae: *quietly* **"...I didn't say that."**

Soo-ho just **smiled.**

And Ji-ae **hated** how warm her face felt.

By the time Ji-ae and Soo-ho finally **reached the campsite**,
they were **met with complete disaster.**

- **The tents were soaked.**
- **Half the snacks were gone.**
- **Someone (JianHao) was being chased by a furious
  Denise.**
- **Debbie was roasting marshmallows... over a burning
  jacket.**

Ji-ae: "…What the hell happened here?"

Denise: "JianHao happened."

JianHao: "IT WASN'T MY FAULT!"

Debbie: "Then whose jacket am I roasting?"

Madeline: "…That's MY jacket."

Silence.

Madeline: "…I'M GOING TO KILL YOU."

Ji-ae watched as **Madeline launched herself at Debbie.**

Ji-ae: "I leave for ONE NIGHT, and you guys start acting like wild animals."

Soo-ho: *smirking* "This is normal for them."

Later that night, **the group finally calmed down** (well, after Denise force-fed JianHao a burnt marshmallow as revenge).

Everyone gathered around the **bonfire**, sharing **funny and embarrassing stories.**

Ji-ae: "…And then I turned around and realized my skirt was tucked into my bag the WHOLE time."

Denise: "Oh my god, not that day."

Debbie: "I WAS THERE. I ALMOST DIED LAUGHING."

Soo-ho: **"...I would've helped you fix it."**

Ji-ae: *blinking* **"...Wait, really?"**

Soo-ho: **"Yeah."**

JianHao: **"This guy is SMOOTH."**

Ji-ae felt her face **heating up.**

Soo-ho just **leaned closer**, whispering—**"I'll always look out for you."**

Ji-ae **nearly choked on air.**

Denise: **"Alright, before we end the night—time for a SURPRISE!"**

Debbie: **"And it's for Ji-ae!"**

Ji-ae: **"...Huh?"**

JianHao: **"Soo-ho planned it."**

Ji-ae: **"WHAT?!"**

She **whipped her head around**, but Soo-ho just gave a **tiny smirk.**

Debbie: **"Lights off, everyone!"**

Suddenly, the bonfire **dimmed**, and the group **stepped back.**

Ji-ae: **"Wait, wait, what's happening?"**

Then—**soft lights flickered on.**

A trail of tiny lanterns **lit up the trees, forming a glowing path.**

And at the end of it... **a small table with a warm drink and a cozy blanket.**

Ji-ae: **"...Did you—?"**

Soo-ho: **"I figured after everything, you deserved a peaceful night."**

Ji-ae **stared at him.**

Soo-ho **held out his hand. "Come with me?"**

Her heart **skipped a beat.**

Ji-ae: **"...Yeah. Okay."**

Ji-ae **followed Soo-ho down the glowing path,** her heartbeat **loud in her ears.**

The others had **stayed behind,** leaving only the soft glow of lanterns, the distant crackling of the bonfire, and the faint hum of night insects.

At the end of the path, **Soo-ho pulled out a chair for her.**

Ji-ae: **"...You really planned all this?"**

Soo-ho: **"Did you think I'd let you spend the night in a cave and not make it up to you?"**

Ji-ae: **"Fair point."**

She sat down, and Soo-ho **placed a warm cup of hot chocolate in front of her.**

Ji-ae: *teasing* **"What, no fancy dinner?"**

Soo-ho: **"You want me to cook? You trying to poison yourself?"**

Ji-ae **laughed.**

For a while, **they just sat there, sipping their drinks.**

Ji-ae **leaned back in her chair, looking up at the sky.**

Ji-ae: **"You know... I never thought I'd like it here."**

Soo-ho: **"Titan Academy?"**

Ji-ae: **"Yeah. I thought it'd just be another school. Nothing special."**

Soo-ho: **"...And now?"**

Ji-ae turned her head to look at him.

Ji-ae: **"...Now, it feels like home."**

Soo-ho's eyes softened.

Soo-ho: "**...I'm glad.**"

Ji-ae smiled, but then—

She felt his hand lightly brush against hers.

She froze.

Soo-ho **didn't move his hand away.**

Ji-ae **slowly turned to him, meeting his gaze.**

Soo-ho: *softly* "**Ji-ae.**"

Her breath hitched.

Was this happening?

Before she could think, Soo-ho gently **intertwined their fingers.**

Ji-ae's heart **pounded.**

Soo-ho: *whispering* "**You're important to me.**"

Ji-ae: "**...I—**"

CRASH!

JianHao: "**OH MY GOD, THEY'RE HOLDING HANDS!!**"

Denise: "**YOU IDIOT, YOU RUINED THE MOMENT!!**"

Ji-ae **nearly fell out of her chair.**

Soo-ho **groaned, covering his face.**

Ji-ae turned to find **JianHao, Denise, Debbie, and Madeline peeking from behind the trees.**

Ji-ae: **"SERIOUSLY?!"**

Debbie: **"IT'S NOT OUR FAULT. WE WANTED TO SEE IF YOU'D FINALLY KISS."**

Ji-ae: **"I'M GOING TO STRANGLE YOU."**

Madeline: **"Worth it."**

Soo-ho, still holding Ji-ae's hand, **sighed deeply.**

Soo-ho: **"…Next time, we're running away."**

Ji-ae: **"Agreed."**

After **kicking their friends out,** Ji-ae and Soo-ho finally had a moment to themselves again.

Ji-ae: *grumbling* **"I swear, one day, I'll actually get to enjoy a moment with you without those idiots spying on us."**

Soo-ho: *smirking* **"You think they'll ever stop?"**

Ji-ae: **"…No."**

Soo-ho **chuckled** and leaned back in his chair, still holding her hand.

Soo-ho: **"You never finished what you were saying earlier."**

Ji-ae blinked.

Ji-ae: **"…What?"**

Soo-ho: *softly* **"When I said you're important to me. You were about to say something."**

Ji-ae's face warmed.

She hesitated, then **squeezed his hand gently.**

Ji-ae: **"…You're important to me too."**

Soo-ho didn't reply right away. He just **stared at her**, his dark eyes reflecting the soft glow of the lanterns.

Ji-ae suddenly felt **so aware** of how close they were.

Soo-ho: *low voice* **"…Good."**

Her heart skipped a beat.

Why did that sound so attractive?!

Soo-ho lifted their intertwined hands and, without breaking eye contact, **pressed a light kiss to her fingers.**

Ji-ae **forgot how to breathe.**

Ji-ae: **"…Soo-ho?"**

Soo-ho: *smirking* **"I like the way you say my name."**

HELP.

Ji-ae **felt like melting into a puddle on the ground.**

Before she could embarrass herself further, **a loud yawn escaped her.**

Soo-ho: **"Tired?"**

Ji-ae: **"…Maybe."**

Soo-ho: *softly* **"Come on, let's get you to bed."**

Soo-ho walked Ji-ae back to her tent, their hands **still linked.**

Ji-ae: *sleepy* **"…Thanks for tonight."**

Soo-ho: **"Get some rest."**

She turned to go inside, but then—

She paused.

Ji-ae: *quietly* **"…Goodnight, Soo-ho."**

She didn't wait for a response. Instead, she quickly slipped into her tent, heart racing.

Outside, Soo-ho stood there for a moment before murmuring—

"...Goodnight, Ji-ae."

he school trip was **almost over,** but there was **one last activity left.**

Denise: **"Alright, listen up! Today, we're doing a trust exercise."**

JianHao: **"That sounds suspicious."**

Debbie: **"It's a classic 'trust fall' game. You have to fall, and your partner catches you."**

Ji-ae: **"...And what happens if they don't catch you?"**

Denise: **"Then you die."**

Madeline: **"You don't DIE, Denise."**

Denise: **"Fine. Then you get emotionally scarred for life."**

Ji-ae **sighed.**

Of course, she was paired with **Soo-ho.**

Ji-ae: *narrowing her eyes* **"You better not let me fall."**

Soo-ho: *smirking* **"Wouldn't dream of it."**

Ji-ae **crossed her arms.** **"...Prove it."**

Soo-ho **chuckled.**

Soo-ho: **"Alright then. Fall."**

Ji-ae hesitated for a moment before **closing her eyes and leaning back.**

Her heart pounded as the ground **rushed toward her—**

But before she could panic, **strong arms caught her effortlessly.**

Soo-ho: *whispering close to her ear* **"Told you I wouldn't let you fall."**

Ji-ae's **eyes snapped open.**

He was **way too close.**

She could feel his warmth, his steady breathing, the way his arms **held her like she was the most important thing in the world.**

Ji-ae: **"...Soo-ho?"**

Soo-ho **just smiled.**

Soo-ho: **"I'll always catch you."**

After what felt like the **longest and most eventful school trip of their lives,** the students of Titan Academy **finally returned.**

Denise: **"I swear, that trip felt like a whole season of a K-drama."**

JianHao: "**And yet, we still have to deal with *actual* school now. Tragic.**"

Ji-ae **sighed as she walked into the classroom, Soo-ho right beside her.**

Everything felt... **different.**

Maybe it was because of **everything** that had happened—the hike, the thunderstorm, the cave, **the moments they shared.**

Ji-ae stole a glance at Soo-ho.

He was **looking at her too.**

Soo-ho: *smirking* "**Miss me already?**"

Ji-ae: *rolling her eyes* "**We literally just spent the entire trip together.**"

Soo-ho: *teasing* "**And yet, you're looking at me like that.**"

Ji-ae: *flustered* "**LIKE WHAT?!**"

Soo-ho: *grinning* "**Like you want to kiss me.**"

HELP.

Ji-ae **nearly choked on air.**

Ji-ae: "**LEE SOO-HO—**"

Before she could yell at him, Denise **suddenly burst into the room, waving her phone.**

Denise: **"GUYS. We have a problem."**

Ji-ae: **"What now?"**

Denise **shoved her phone in their faces.**

Denise: **"LOOK AT THIS!"**

Ji-ae and Soo-ho leaned in.

On the screen was a **brand-new school announcement—**

A **huge** event was coming up.

Madeline: **"The school is throwing... A MASQUERADE BALL?!?"**

JianHao: *grinning* **"Ooooh, fancy."**

Debbie: *deadpan* **"No, *stressful*."**

Ji-ae blinked. **A ball?!**

Denise: **"Who are you guys going with?!"**

Ji-ae: **"I... I don't know?"**

Denise: **"WHAT DO YOU MEAN YOU DON'T KNOW?!"**

Ji-ae felt a little flustered. **Would Soo-ho ask her?**

Soo-ho, on the other hand, **looked way too relaxed.**

Soo-ho: *leaning close* **"Waiting for someone to ask you?"**

Ji-ae: *narrowing her eyes* **"Are you going to or not?"**

Soo-ho **chuckled.**

Soo-ho: **"Guess you'll just have to wait and see."**

The moment the **Masquerade Ball** was announced, Titan Academy **descended into chaos.**

Denise: **"OKAY. We have approximately four days to find the perfect outfits, pick our masks, and most importantly—GET A DATE."**

Debbie: **"That last part seems optional."**

Denise: **"NO, IT'S NOT."**

JianHao: **"Relax. It's not that serious."**

Denise: **"SAYS THE ONE WHO NEVER STRESSES ABOUT ANYTHING."**

Ji-ae, meanwhile, was **only half-listening.**

She stole a glance at Soo-ho, who was just **sitting there, smirking like he knew something nobody else did.**

Ji-ae: *narrowing her eyes* **"You haven't asked me yet."**

Soo-ho: *innocently* **"Asked you what?"**

Ji-ae: **"To the ball, obviously!"**

Soo-ho leaned closer, voice **dangerously low.**

Soo-ho: **"Do I really need to ask?"**

Ji-ae's heart **skipped a beat.**

Soo-ho: *grinning* **"I thought it was obvious you'd be going with me."**

Ji-ae: **"Lee Soo-ho, I swear—"**

Soo-ho: *chuckling* **"Fine. Ji-ae, will you go to the Masquerade Ball with me?"**

Ji-ae **crossed her arms.**

Ji-ae: **"I'll think about it."**

Soo-ho: **"What?!"**

Ji-ae: *smirking* **"Maybe I want to keep YOU waiting this time."**

Two days before the ball, Ji-ae, Denise, Debbie, and Madeline were at the mall looking for **dresses and masks.**

Denise: **"We need to be the best-dressed people there."**

Debbie: **"I still don't get why this is such a big deal."**

Ji-ae, however, was **lost in thought.**

She hadn't told anyone, but...

She planned to surprise Soo-ho.

Instead of **going with him as expected,** she was going to **keep her identity hidden.**

Denise: *snapping fingers in front of Ji-ae* **"HELLO? Earth to Ji-ae?"**

Ji-ae: **"Huh? What?"**

Denise: *grinning* **"I just found your perfect dress."**

Ji-ae turned—and **her breath caught.**

It was a stunning, floor-length **black silk gown with subtle gold embroidery.**

Ji-ae: **"...Okay, maybe you're actually a genius."**

Denise: **"I KNOW."**

Titan Academy's **gymnasium had been completely transformed.**

Golden chandeliers, glittering lights, and elegant decorations made it feel **like a fairytale.**

Soo-ho stood near the entrance, dressed in a **sharp black suit with a matching mask.**

JianHao: **"Dude, where's your date?"**

Soo-ho: "**She's coming.**"

JianHao: "**...Are you sure?**"

Soo-ho frowned. **Was Ji-ae actually ditching him?!**

But then—

A figure entered the ballroom.

Soo-ho **immediately recognized her.**

The way she walked, the way the candlelight reflected in her eyes...

Ji-ae.

Dressed in black silk, wearing a delicate gold mask that covered just enough of her face to make her **mysterious.**

Soo-ho's breath hitched.

Soo-ho: "**Damn.**"

JianHao: "**Oh, yeah, you're down BAD.**"

Soo-ho ignored him and **started walking toward her.**

Ji-ae: "**You found me fast.**"

Soo-ho: "**I'd find you anywhere.**"

Ji-ae bit her lip to hide her smile.

Soo-ho: *offering his hand* **"Dance with me?"**

Ji-ae hesitated... then placed her hand in his.

As they moved to the dance floor, Soo-ho leaned in and **whispered against her ear—**

Soo-ho: **"You look breathtaking."**

Ji-ae: **"You don't look too bad yourself."**

Soo-ho: **"You planned to hide from me all night, didn't you?"**

Ji-ae: *grinning* **"Maybe."**

Soo-ho: **"Too bad. You're stuck with me now."**

Ji-ae: **"I think I'm okay with that."**

As Ji-ae and Soo-ho swayed to the soft melody, **the rest of the world faded away.**

Soo-ho's hand was **firm yet gentle** against her waist, and the way his fingers brushed against hers sent **shivers down her spine.**

Ji-ae: **"This night feels unreal."**

Soo-ho: *smirking* **"Because you're dancing with the most handsome guy in school?"**

Ji-ae: *rolling her eyes* **"Because it's rare for Titan Academy to have a night this peaceful."**

Soo-ho chuckled, his gaze never leaving her.

Soo-ho: **"I was talking about you."**

Ji-ae: **"What?"**

Soo-ho: **"You're the one who doesn't feel real."**

Ji-ae's breath hitched. **That was dangerous.**

Soo-ho had a way of saying things that left her heart **spiraling out of control.**

And then—**the song slowed even more.**

Ji-ae suddenly felt **way too aware** of the space—or lack thereof—between them.

She swallowed.

Ji-ae: **"You know... it's crazy how much has changed since we first met."**

Soo-ho: **"Yeah. Back then, you could barely stand me."**

Ji-ae: *smirking* **"Still can't sometimes."**

Soo-ho laughed softly, his grip tightening around her waist.

Soo-ho: **"And yet, here you are. Stuck with me on the dance floor."**

Ji-ae: **"Maybe I don't mind being stuck with you."**

Soo-ho: **"Good."**

And then...

The music **faded into silence.**

For a moment, neither of them moved.

Soo-ho's gaze flickered to Ji-ae's lips—**just for a second.**

Ji-ae felt her pulse race.

And before she could **overthink it**, she whispered—

Ji-ae: **"Soo-ho."**

That was all it took.

He **closed the distance.**

It wasn't rushed.

It wasn't hesitant.

It was **soft, warm, and full of every unspoken feeling** that had been building up between them.

The world **disappeared.**

It was just **them.**

Just **this moment.**

And when they finally pulled away, Ji-ae was breathless.

Soo-ho smirked, brushing a strand of hair from her face.

Soo-ho: **"Took us long enough, huh?"**

Ji-ae: *cheeks burning* **"Shut up."**

Soo-ho: **"Never."**

And just like that—

Titan Academy's **Masquerade Ball** became **the night everything changed.** ♥??

Ji-ae barely had time to process what just happened. **They kissed.**

She kissed Soo-ho.

Or—**he kissed her?**

Or **they both kissed each other?!**

Her brain was **malfunctioning.**

Meanwhile, Soo-ho was just standing there, hands in his pockets, **looking way too smug for someone who just turned her world upside down.**

Soo-ho: **"Speechless?"**

Ji-ae: *glaring* **"No!"**

Soo-ho: *raising an eyebrow* **"Really? Because you haven't said anything for the past two minutes."**

Ji-ae: *stammering* **"I—I was just processing!"**

Soo-ho: **"Mhm. Processing how amazing I am?"**

Ji-ae: **"No! Processing why I didn't punch you!"**

Soo-ho: *grinning* **"I'd say it's because deep down, you liked it."**

Ji-ae: **"I—"** She **froze.**

Because she had **no comeback.**

Soo-ho **laughed.** Like, a full-on **"I just won"** laugh.

Before she could **properly murder him**, Denise and Debbie suddenly **appeared out of nowhere** and grabbed Ji-ae by the arm.

Denise: **"EXCUSE ME, MA'AM. WE NEED TO TALK."**

Debbie: **"RIGHT NOW."**

Soo-ho: *chuckling* **"Don't keep them waiting, sweetheart."**

Ji-ae: *glaring* **"I will end you."**

Soo-ho: "**You can try.**"

Ugh.

This boy was **too much.**

Ji-ae was done.

Done **being flustered** every time Soo-ho smirked at her.
Done **getting teased** like she was some helpless, lovesick
fool.
Done **losing** in this game.

It was time to **flip the script.**

So when she saw Soo-ho standing near the refreshments
table, **looking all smug like he owned the world**, she took
a deep breath, straightened her posture, and **activated her
inner menace.**

She casually strolled over, picking up a drink, and gave
him a **sweet, innocent smile.**

Ji-ae: "**Soo-ho.**"

Soo-ho: *smirking* "**Ji-ae.**"

Ji-ae: "**I was thinking.**"

Soo-ho: "**Dangerous.**"

Ji-ae: *ignoring him* "**That kiss we had...**"

Soo-ho: *raises an eyebrow* **"Oh? What about it?"**

Ji-ae: *tilting her head, pretending to think* **"I just realized..."**

Soo-ho leaned in slightly, curious.

Ji-ae: *grinning* **"It was... cute."**

Soo-ho: *blinking* **"Cute?"**

Ji-ae: *nodding, sipping her drink* **"Yeah. Like, you know, when a puppy accidentally licks your face?"**

Soo-ho: **"...Excuse me?"**

Ji-ae: *innocently* **"You know! It's like, you think it's gonna be all grand and swoon-worthy, but in the end, it's just... kind of adorable. Like, 'aww, look at you, trying so hard.'"**

Soo-ho **stared.**

Denise and Debbie, who had been eavesdropping, **slapped their hands over their mouths to stop from laughing.**

Soo-ho: *narrowing his eyes* **"Are you saying my kiss was like... a puppy lick?"**

Ji-ae: *grinning* **"Don't feel bad! It was a very nice puppy lick."**

Debbie **choked on her drink.**

Denise **wheezed.**

Soo-ho: *crossing his arms* "**Oh, you're asking for it now.**"

Ji-ae: "**Asking for what? A treat? Belly rubs?**"

Soo-ho: "**Ji-ae—**"

Ji-ae: *placing a hand on his shoulder, mockingly serious* "**It's okay, Soo-ho. Not everyone can be naturally smooth. But don't worry! If you ever want lessons, I—**"

Before she could finish, Soo-ho **took a step forward**, closing the distance between them.

His smirk returned.

Soo-ho: *softly* "**You sure you wanna challenge me?**"

Ji-ae felt her face heat up. **Uh-oh.**

Denise: *whispering* "**Abort mission, Ji-ae. ABORT.**"

Debbie: "**He's turning the tables! RETREAT!**"

Ji-ae: *clearing her throat* "**Uh... yeah! What, scared you won't win?**"

Soo-ho: "**Oh, I always win. But just so you know, Ji-ae... the next time I kiss you, I'll make sure you never call it 'cute' again.**"

Ji-ae: *malfunctioning* "**...I hate you.**"

Soo-ho: *grinning* "**You love me.**"

Ji-ae: **"IN YOUR DREAMS."**

Soo-ho: **"Oh, definitely."**

Ji-ae turned on her heel and stormed off while **Denise and Debbie screamed into their hands.**

Denise: **"HE'S GONNA DESTROY YOU."**

Debbie: **"YOU POKED THE BEAST."**

Ji-ae: **"NO REGRETS."**

But deep down, she knew...

She was so doomed.

The final day at **Titan Academy** had arrived.

The hallways were filled with students **signing uniforms, taking last-minute pictures, and making promises to stay in touch.** Excitement buzzed through the air, but there was also a bittersweet feeling.

For Ji-ae, it felt **unreal.**

She sat in the **graduation hall**, surrounded by her classmates, dressed in her cap and gown. The stage was set, teachers were making speeches, and students were already whispering about their summer plans.

But Ji-ae couldn't focus.

Her eyes drifted to **Soo-ho**, sitting just a few seats away.

He was playing with the tassel on his cap, looking effortlessly cool, but when he caught her staring, he smirked.

Soo-ho: **"Getting emotional already?"**

Ji-ae: *rolling her eyes* **"Pfft. No."**

Soo-ho: *grinning* **"You sure? You're kinda looking at me like you'll miss me."**

Ji-ae: **"Don't flatter yourself."**

Soo-ho: **"Too late."**

Before Ji-ae could fire back, the principal's voice echoed through the speakers.

Principal: **"Graduating class of Titan Academy... congratulations!"**

Cheers erupted as students stood, caps in hand, ready for the final moment.

Principal: **"On the count of three... throw your caps into the air!"**

3... 2... 1!

Hats flew up, voices shouted, laughter rang through the air.

It was chaos. It was loud. It was **perfect.**

Ji-ae laughed as Denise tackled her into a hug, **Debbie screamed in excitement, and Madeline wiped away dramatic fake tears.**

Then, suddenly, a **warm hand** grabbed hers.

Ji-ae turned, **heart skipping a beat.**

Soo-ho stood there, **watching her, smiling.**

Soo-ho: **"Come with me."**

Without waiting for her to answer, he **gently pulled her through the crowd, past the students celebrating, past the teachers congratulating them, until they reached a quiet spot near the garden.**

The excitement of graduation faded into the background.

It was just the **two of them.**

Ji-ae: *softly* **"What are we doing here?"**

Soo-ho: *shrugging* **"Just wanted a moment. Just us."**

Ji-ae: *teasing* **"What, you gonna cry?"**

Soo-ho: *chuckling* **"You wish."**

They stood there for a moment, the realization sinking in.

They were **done with high school.**
This was **the end of an era.**

Ji-ae bit her lip. **"So... what happens now?"**

Soo-ho was quiet for a second, then he **took a step closer.**

Soo-ho: **"We move forward. Together."**

Ji-ae felt her heart race.

Soo-ho: **"No more stupid bets, no more teasing—"**

Ji-ae: *grinning* **"I kinda like the teasing."**

Soo-ho: *chuckling* **"Fine. A little teasing. But... mostly this."**

And before Ji-ae could process what he meant, he **leaned in and kissed her.**

It wasn't rushed. It wasn't a stolen moment.

It was slow, deep, and filled with **everything they had been too stubborn to say.**

Ji-ae melted into it, fingers curling into his graduation gown as he cupped her face, like he had been **waiting for this.**

When they finally pulled away, Soo-ho grinned.

Soo-ho: **"Still think my kisses are like puppy licks?"**

Ji-ae: **"Shut up."**

Soo-ho: **"That's what I thought."**

Ji-ae rolled her eyes, but she was **smiling.**

Because yeah, they were graduating.
Yeah, things were changing.
But **this?**

This was just the beginning. ♥??

After graduation, reality hit **fast.**

Titan Academy was **over,** and life was **officially changing.**

Most students were talking about **college, travel plans, or taking a break**, but Ji-ae and Soo-ho? **They had different plans.**

"Wanna Move In With Me?"

It happened one night, a few days after graduation.

Ji-ae and Soo-ho were sitting on a rooftop, **watching the stars, eating ramen straight from the cup, and arguing over which flavor was better.**

Ji-ae: **"Kimchi ramen is superior, admit it."**

Soo-ho: **"No way. Spicy beef is the GOAT."**

Ji-ae: *rolling her eyes* **"Your taste buds are broken."**

Soo-ho: *smirking* **"And yet, you still kissed me."**

Ji-ae: *choking on ramen* **"Shut up."**

Soo-ho laughed, reaching over to wipe a stray noodle off her cheek.

Then, **out of nowhere**, he said—

Soo-ho: **"Move in with me."**

Ji-ae blinked. **"Wait... what?"**

Soo-ho: **"You heard me."**

Ji-ae: **"You're joking, right?"**

Soo-ho: *grinning* **"Do I look like I'm joking?"**

Ji-ae stared at him, waiting for him to say "Just kidding!" or "Gotcha!" but **he didn't.**

He just **looked at her**, serious and soft at the same time.

Soo-ho: **"I want to wake up next to you every day, argue over ramen flavors, and steal your hoodies."**

Ji-ae: *narrowing her eyes* **"Why would you steal my hoodies?"**

Soo-ho: *smirking* **"Because they smell like you."**

Ji-ae: *heart malfunctioning* **"...You're unfair."**

Soo-ho: "**I know. But is that a yes?**"

Ji-ae sighed dramatically. "**Ugh, fine. But if you leave the toilet seat up, I'm moving out.**"

Soo-ho grinned. "**Deal.**"

Moving in = Absolute Chaos

A week later, **it was official.**

Ji-ae stood in their new apartment, **hands on her hips, staring at the disaster that was unpacking.**

Ji-ae: "**WHY do you have so many black shirts?!**"

Soo-ho: *shrugging* "**I like black.**"

Ji-ae: *holding up three identical hoodies* "**This is a sickness.**"

Soo-ho: "**Says the girl with ten different scented candles.**"

Ji-ae: "**EXCUSE ME?! Scented candles are a necessity. And at least I have a variety.**"

Soo-ho: "**Oh yeah? And so is my gaming setup.**"

Ji-ae: *gasps* "**You did NOT just compare scented candles to a gaming setup.**"

Soo-ho: *grinning* "**I did. What are you gonna do about it?**"

Ji-ae: **"I'm confiscating your controller."**

Soo-ho: **"You wouldn't dare."**

Ji-ae: *smirking* **"Watch me."**

And just like that, **living together turned into a daily war of pranks, late-night ramen, stolen hoodies, and the sweetest kind of chaos.**

But Also... Soft Moments ♥?

Of course, it wasn't **just teasing and bickering.**

There were nights when they curled up on the couch, Soo-ho's arm around Ji-ae as they watched some dumb movie.

There were mornings when Ji-ae woke up to the smell of pancakes, only to find Soo-ho in the kitchen **(with flour on his nose, struggling to flip a pancake).**

There were lazy Sundays when Ji-ae would be **reading on the balcony,** and Soo-ho would just sit beside her, **watching her instead of the book.**

Soo-ho: **"You're prettier than the sunrise."**

Ji-ae: *blushing* **"SHUT UP."**

Soo-ho: **"What? Just speaking facts."**

Ji-ae: *hiding her face in her book* "**I hate you.**"

Soo-ho: *grinning* "**Nah, you love me.**"

And the worst part?

He was right.

It had been a few months since they moved in together, and life was **pretty much perfect.**

Except for one thing.

Ji-ae: "**Soo-ho, my parents keep asking when you'll visit.**"

Soo-ho: "**Oh... like visit, visit?**"

Ji-ae: *raising an eyebrow* "**What other kind of visit is there?**"

Soo-ho: *nervous chuckle* "**Do they... like me?**"

Ji-ae: *grinning* "**They will once they meet you.**"

Soo-ho: "**That doesn't sound very convincing.**"

Ji-ae: "**It wasn't meant to be.**"

Soo-ho: *panicking* "**Ji-ae—**"

Ji-ae: *laughing* "**Relax, they'll love you.**"

Soo-ho wasn't convinced. **Meeting Ji-ae's parents in India was a BIG DEAL.**

But then she said—

Ji-ae: **"We can go during Ganesh Chaturthi."**

Soo-ho blinked. **"Wait, the festival with all the lights, dancing, and crazy celebrations?"**

Ji-ae: **"Yup! It'll be fun!"**

Soo-ho: **"Fun? Or absolute chaos?"**

Ji-ae: **"Both. Definitely both."**

Soo-ho sighed, but when Ji-ae looked at him with **that smile**—the one that made his heart **do a backflip**—he knew he had no choice.

Soo-ho: **"Fine. Let's book the tickets."**

The Flight to India ✈?

A week later, they were on a **long-haul flight to India.**

Soo-ho was chilling, watching a movie, when suddenly—**TURBULENCE.**

Ji-ae, who had been half-asleep, **immediately shot up, gripping the armrest.**

Then, without thinking, she **grabbed Soo-ho's hand.**

Ji-ae: *whispering* "**Oh my god.**"

Soo-ho: *looking at her* "**Are you okay?**"

Ji-ae: *nodding rapidly, still holding his hand* "**Yeah. Totally fine. Super fine. Just... turbulence is stupid.**"

Soo-ho: "**You're scared of turbulence?**"

Ji-ae: "**NO.**"*pauses* "**...Maybe.**"

Soo-ho bit back a grin. **Ji-ae never admitted when she was scared.**

So instead of teasing, he **gently squeezed her hand.**

Soo-ho: "**Hey. I got you, okay?**"

Ji-ae looked at him, and suddenly, **the turbulence didn't seem so bad.**

She sighed and leaned her head on his shoulder.

Ji-ae: "**You better not let go.**"

Soo-ho: *softly* "**Never.**"

Landing in India ??

As soon as they landed, Ji-ae was **excitedly pointing at everything.**

Ji-ae: "Okay, first rule—ALWAYS bargain with auto drivers. If they say 200 rupees, you say 100."

Soo-ho: "Wait, there are bargaining rules?"

Ji-ae: "DUH. Also, don't drink water from just anywhere. Stick to bottled water."

Soo-ho: *nodding* "Got it."

Ji-ae: "And—OH MY GOD, LOOK! PANI PURI!!"

Soo-ho: "What is pani puri?"

Ji-ae: *gasping* "OH, YOU'RE ABOUT TO EXPERIENCE HEAVEN."

And just like that, **their India trip had begun.**

Ji-ae and Soo-ho stood in front of her family home in India.

Soo-ho: *whispering* "Tell me again. What do I call them?"

Ji-ae: "Just be polite. Mom is 'eomma,' Dad is 'papa.' And don't embarrass me."

Soo-ho: *offended* "I never embarrass you!"

Ji-ae: *deadpan* "You literally tripped over air at the airport."

Before he could argue, the door swung open.

Ji-ae's mom, a graceful Korean woman with a warm smile, pulled her into a tight hug.

Ji-ae's Mom: "Ji-ae! Aigoo, you look so thin! Are you eating enough?"

Ji-ae: *laughing* "Eomma, I eat just fine."

Then her dad appeared, arms crossed.

Ji-ae's Dad: "Soo-ho, right?"

Soo-ho: *bowing slightly* "Yes, sir."

Ji-ae's Dad: *eyeing him* "So, you're the guy who stole my daughter's heart."

Soo-ho: *sweating* "I—uh—she stole mine first!"

Ji-ae: *facepalming* "Oh my god."

Her dad suddenly smirked.

Ji-ae's Dad: "Hah! I like him."

Ji-ae: "WHAT—"

Ji-ae's Mom: *laughing* "Come in, come in!"

Soo-ho exhaled in relief. One hurdle down.

At dinner, Ji-ae's dad started asking her something in Gujarati.

Ji-ae responded flawlessly, switching languages effortlessly.

Soo-ho froze.

His ears turned red.

Ji-ae: *casually talking in Gujarati* "Kem cho, papa? Maja ma?" (How are you, Dad? Are you well?)

Soo-ho: ...oh. OH.

Ji-ae's Dad: *laughing* "Tari maa ne puch! Atyare to hu maja ma chu." (Ask your mom! Right now, I'm doing well.)

Soo-ho: *whispering* "What... was that?"

Ji-ae: *confused* "What?"

Soo-ho: "That. That language. Say something else."

Ji-ae: "Why?"

Soo-ho: *grinning* "Because it sounds insanely hot."

Ji-ae: "...EXCUSE ME?"

Soo-ho: *leaning closer* "I think I need lessons."

Ji-ae: *narrowing her eyes* "Are you serious right now?"

Soo-ho: "One hundred percent."

Ji-ae's Dad: *cutting in* "Teach him something useful. Like how to ask for more food."

Soo-ho: "Yes, exactly! Priorities!"

Ji-ae rolled her eyes but smirked.

Ji-ae: *teasing* "Fine. Repeat after me: 'Hu tane prem karu chu.'"

Soo-ho: *attempting* "Hu... tane... prem... karu chu?"

Ji-ae: *grinning* "Good job. Now you just said 'I love you' in Gujarati."

Soo-ho: "Wait, what—"

Ji-ae's parents BURST out laughing.

Soo-ho: "JI-AE!!"

Ji-ae: *innocently* "What? You wanted to learn."

Soo-ho: *grinning* "Oh, you're SO going to regret that."

And just like that, the chaos began.

The streets of **Mumbai** were alive with **color, music, and the scent of delicious street food.** Ji-ae and Soo-ho stood amidst the buzzing crowd, surrounded by lanterns, flower garlands, and the rhythmic beats of dhol drums.

And **Soo-ho…** was wearing a **kurta.**

A deep blue, **silk kurta with gold embroidery.**

Ji-ae: *grinning* **"Well, well, well… look at you, Mr. Bollywood Prince."**

Soo-ho: *adjusting his sleeves* **"I feel like I'm wearing a dress."**

Ji-ae: *laughing* **"It's called a kurta, you uncultured swine."**

Soo-ho: *smirking* **"Say that again in Gujarati."**

Ji-ae: *rolling her eyes* **"Not happening."**

Her **parents chuckled** as they guided them toward the temple. The statue of **Lord Ganesha** was adorned with flowers and candles, and the air buzzed with **devotion and energy.**

Ji-ae clasped her hands in prayer. Soo-ho, watching her, hesitated before copying her movements.

Ji-ae: *softly* **"You can just wish for something in your heart."**

Soo-ho closed his eyes.

Soo-ho's Wish: *"Please… let me have Ji-ae forever."*

After the prayers, it was time for **Garba.**

Ji-ae **lit up with excitement.Soo-ho? Not so much.**

Ji-ae: *grabbing his hand* **"Come on, I'll teach you!"**

Soo-ho: **"I think my soul left my body when I saw those spins."**

Ji-ae: *laughing* **"You'll be fine! It's just a simple step. Look—"**

She **spun gracefully, her lehenga twirling.** Soo-ho, hypnotized, **barely remembered how to breathe.**

Ji-ae: **"Now you try."**

Soo-ho took a deep breath... and **tried.**

And FAILED. **Miserably.**

Instead of **gracefully spinning, he tripped over his own feet, crashed into someone, and almost took down the entire dance circle.**

Soo-ho: *flat on the ground* **"...I think I broke my dignity."**

Ji-ae: *dying of laughter* **"OH MY GOD, YOU'RE HOPELESS."**

Soo-ho: *grumbling* **"At least I looked good failing."**

Ji-ae helped him up, **wiping tears of laughter from her eyes.**

Ji-ae: **"You really tried."**

Soo-ho: *grinning* **"Anything for you."**

And just like that... her **heart melted.**

After the **Garba disaster,** they escaped to a quieter street lined with glowing lanterns. The soft flicker of lights reflected in Ji-ae's eyes.

Soo-ho: **"You love this, don't you?"**

Ji-ae: **"I grew up with this. It feels like home."**

Soo-ho reached out and **tucked a stray strand of hair behind her ear.**

Soo-ho: *softly* **"Then I guess... I'm home too."**

Ji-ae's breath hitched.

The world around them faded.

Then, **Soo-ho leaned in.**

And Ji-ae... **closed the distance.**

A slow, deep, breathtaking **kiss.** Under the festival lights, surrounded by the echoes of distant music, the warmth of their love **felt like the only thing that mattered.**

Soo-ho pulled away slightly, **resting his forehead against hers.**

Soo-ho: *whispering* **"Hu tane prem karu chu."**

Ji-ae: *stunned* **"...You remembered that?"**

Soo-ho: *grinning* **"How could I forget?"**

Ji-ae laughed, shaking her head.

Ji-ae: *smirking* **"Alright. Now you're REALLY getting Gujarati lessons."**

And with that, their **love story in India** had only just begun.

Living together brought countless little moments that Ji-ae cherished. She loved waking up to the sight of Soo-ho's peaceful face, his hair adorably messy from sleep. She loved how he always made her morning coffee, even though she knew he wasn't a morning person. She loved their grocery shopping trips, where Soo-ho would sigh dramatically every time she picked up another unnecessary snack.

"Ji-ae, do we really need three different kinds of chips?" he asked, raising an eyebrow.

She grinned. "Yes, because sometimes I'm in a sweet mood, sometimes I want spicy, and sometimes I just need plain salted!"

He shook his head but placed the chips in the cart anyway. "You're impossible."

"And yet, you love me."

Soo-ho glanced at her, a small smile playing on his lips.
"Yeah. I do."

Her heart melted every time he said it so effortlessly, like it
was the most natural thing in the world.

One evening, they were curled up on the couch watching a
movie when Ji-ae absentmindedly said, "I could stay like
this forever."

Soo-ho, who had been running his fingers through her
hair, paused for a moment before murmuring, "Then let's
make it forever."

Ji-ae sat up, blinking at him. "What?"

Soo-ho's expression was unreadable, but his eyes held
something intense. "I mean it, Ji-ae. I want us to be
together. Always."

Her heart pounded. "Are you... are you saying—?"

He took her hand, pressing it against his chest. "I don't
have a ring yet, and maybe it's too soon, but..." He exhaled,
his lips curling into a soft smile. "One day, I want to marry
you."

Ji-ae's breath hitched. The idea of marriage had never
crossed her mind so soon, but when she thought about
it—thought about spending the rest of her life with Soo-
ho—it didn't scare her. It felt right.

She threw her arms around his neck, squeezing him tightly. "Then one day, I'll say yes."

Soo-ho chuckled, his arms tightening around her waist. "That's good enough for me."

Though they weren't engaged yet, things between them only grew more serious. They started talking about their future more—about where they wanted to live, what kind of home they'd have, even silly things like how many pets they'd get.

"Three dogs and two cats," Ji-ae announced one night as they lay in bed.

Soo-ho raised an eyebrow. "That's a zoo."

Ji-ae pouted. "Fine, two dogs and one cat?"

Soo-ho smirked. "We'll negotiate when the time comes."

Every moment felt like a new adventure, even in the smallest things. Grocery shopping, lazy Sunday mornings, even arguing over who had to do the dishes—it all became special because they were together.

One day, Ji-ae came home to find Soo-ho standing in the kitchen, looking hesitant.

"What's wrong?" she asked, slipping off her shoes.

He turned to her, rubbing the back of his neck. "I was thinking... we should get a bigger place."

Ji-ae blinked. "Why?"

Soo-ho shrugged. "Well... we're going to be together for a long time. We might as well start planning for it now."

Ji-ae's heart fluttered. Moving in together had already been a big step, but thinking about a real home—a place they built together—felt even bigger.

"You really see that far ahead with me?" she asked softly.

Soo-ho stepped closer, tucking a strand of hair behind her ear. "I've seen our future since the day I met you."

Ji-ae laughed, warmth spreading through her chest. "Then let's find our dream home."

As the months passed, Ji-ae and Soo-ho found a cozy apartment, one with a big window where the sunlight streamed in every morning. It became their little world—a place filled with laughter, quiet mornings, late-night talks, and endless love.

And as Ji-ae curled up against Soo-ho one evening, watching the city lights twinkle outside their window, she knew—this was just the beginning. Their story was far from over. It was only the start of their forever.

Months passed, and Ji-ae and Soo-ho settled into their new apartment, turning it into a home filled with warmth and love. Every morning, they woke up tangled in each other's arms, and every night, they fell asleep knowing they had someone to come home to.

But as perfect as things seemed, life had a way of testing even the strongest love.

One evening, Soo-ho came home later than usual, his expression tense. Ji-ae, who had been waiting for him with dinner ready, immediately noticed something was off.

"What's wrong?" she asked, setting down her chopsticks.

Soo-ho sighed, running a hand through his hair. "My father called."

Ji-ae stiffened. She knew Soo-ho's relationship with his father was complicated. "What did he say?"

"He wants me to come back to America." Soo-ho's voice was calm, but Ji-ae could sense the storm brewing beneath it. "He says I've wasted enough time here, that I should focus on my future."

Ji-ae swallowed hard, her heart sinking. "And... what do you want?"

Soo-ho looked at her, his gaze steady. "I want to stay here. With you."

Relief washed over her, but it was quickly replaced by concern. "But what about your career? Your dreams?"

Soo-ho reached across the table, taking her hand. "My dreams have changed, Ji-ae. Before, I wanted to be successful, to prove myself. But now... my dream is a life with you."

Ji-ae felt tears prick her eyes. "Soo-ho..."

He squeezed her hand gently. "But I won't lie. My father won't stop pressuring me. And I don't want this to become something that puts a strain on us."

Ji-ae took a deep breath. "Then we face it together." She gave him a small, determined smile. "I'm not going anywhere, Soo-ho. We'll figure this out."

For a moment, he just stared at her—then he let out a soft chuckle, pulling her into his arms. "How did I get so lucky?"

Ji-ae hugged him tightly. "I ask myself the same thing every day."

The days that followed weren't easy. Soo-ho struggled with the weight of his father's words, but Ji-ae never left his side.

One evening, as they sat on the balcony, Soo-ho suddenly said, "Let's go on a trip."

Ji-ae blinked. "Huh?"

"Let's go somewhere. Just the two of us." He turned to her with a small smile. "I think we need it."

Ji-ae grinned. "Where do you want to go?"

"Somewhere peaceful. Somewhere where it's just us."

And so, a week later, they found themselves in a quiet seaside town, walking along the shore as the waves lapped at their feet.

Ji-ae looked up at Soo-ho, watching the way the wind ruffled his hair. "You look happier."

He smiled, lacing his fingers with hers. "I am."

She squeezed his hand. "Then that's all that matters."

Soo-ho pulled her closer, resting his forehead against hers. "I love you, Ji-ae."

She smiled, her heart full. "I love you too."

And as the waves whispered their secrets to the shore, Ji-ae knew—no matter what challenges came their way, their love would always endure.

One day,

Soo-ho adjusted his tie nervously as he sat in the sleek, modern office of MOVE Entertainment. His heart pounded in his chest as he faced the executives across the table. This was it—the moment that could change his life forever.

"Lee Soo-ho," the director said, flipping through his portfolio. "Your audition was impressive. We believe you have great potential."

Soo-ho held his breath.

"We'd like to offer you a position as the newest member of ASTRO."

His eyes widened. "R-really?"

The director smiled. "Yes. And from now on, your stage name will be Cha Eun-woo."

Soo-ho exhaled in disbelief. He did it. He actually did it!

Two weeks later

Soo-ho was on his way to his first official ASTRO meeting. He stepped into the sleek rehearsal room, where his new bandmates greeted him warmly. Everything was happening so fast, but he was ready.

Then, the door burst open.

"Alright, boys!" a familiar voice called. "Let's get to work!"

Soo-ho turned around, and his jaw dropped.

Ji-ae stood in the doorway, holding a clipboard, dressed in an official MOVE Entertainment blazer. She grinned at him.

"J-Ji-ae?" he stammered. "What are you—?"

She smirked. "Surprise. I'm your new manager."

Soo-ho blinked. Then again. His brain short-circuited.

"You're... what?"

"Your. New. Manager." Ji-ae crossed her arms. "You think I was just gonna let you have all the fun without me?"

Soo-ho was speechless. His members chuckled in amusement.

Ji-ae stepped closer, poking his chest playfully. "You better work hard, Cha Eun-woo. Because I'm gonna make sure you become the biggest idol ever."

Soo-ho groaned, running a hand through his hair. "Oh god, this is gonna be a disaster."

Ji-ae smirked. "No, babe. This is gonna be *amazing*."

And just like that, their new adventure began. ??

Soo-ho was still processing the *shock of the century* when his new bandmates burst out laughing.

MJ clapped his hands. "Wait, wait—*she's* your manager?! Oh, this is *gold!*"

JinJin smirked. "I thought managers were supposed to be *professional*. This one looks like she's about to bully her own artist."

Ji-ae shot him a smug look. "Oh, don't worry. I *am* professional. But I'm also his biggest nightmare."

Soo-ho groaned. "I knew it."

Rocky chuckled. "Wow, we've barely debuted together and you're already whipped, Cha Eun-woo."

Sanha gasped dramatically. "Wait—does this mean we have to listen to her too?!"

Ji-ae grinned. "Oh, absolutely." She flipped through her clipboard. "And speaking of which, Sanha, you're *late* to dance practice tomorrow. So guess what? Extra training."

Sanha paled. "W-WHAT? HOW DID YOU EVEN KNOW?!"

Moonbin shook his head, laughing. "Man, this is going to be *fun.*"

Ji-ae turned back to Soo-ho and patted his shoulder. "Alright, star boy. I'll let you soak in your emotions, but starting tomorrow, we're on a strict schedule. No slacking, no whining, and definitely no flirting during practice."

Soo-ho narrowed his eyes. "No flirting? With *who*?"

Ji-ae smirked. "With *me.*"

The ASTRO members erupted in *chaotic howling.*

JinJin wiped fake tears. "I love her already."

MJ pretended to faint. "This is the best thing that's ever happened to ASTRO."

Soo-ho groaned, covering his face. "I should've known you'd make my idol life a living hell."

Ji-ae grinned and leaned closer. "Oh, you love it."

And he *really* did.

The Downfall of Cha Eun-woo (a.k.a. Soo-ho's Suffering)

The next morning, Soo-ho showed up at the practice room, expecting a *normal* training session.

He should've known better.

Ji-ae stood in the middle of the room, clipboard in hand, looking way too smug for his liking.

"Alright, everyone," she called, "since *someone*—" her eyes landed directly on Soo-ho "—has been slacking off on vocal warm-ups, we'll be starting today with *extra* vocal exercises."

Soo-ho narrowed his eyes. "I *don't* slack off."

"Oh?" Ji-ae raised an eyebrow. "Then sing *right now.*"

"Fine." Soo-ho took a deep breath, preparing to sing.

Ji-ae cut him off. "But do it while doing *50 squats.*"

The ASTRO members *lost it.*

MJ fell to the floor laughing. "*Fifty?!* Manager-nim, have mercy!"

Sanha was practically in tears. "This is better than a drama."

JinJin smirked. "Go on, Soo-ho. Show us how *dedicated* you are."

Soo-ho shot Ji-ae a *death glare.* "I. Hate. You."

Ji-ae grinned. "No you don't. Now start."

Groaning, Soo-ho began doing squats while singing, his voice cracking halfway.

Ji-ae *smirked* and made a note on her clipboard. "*Unacceptable. Redo it tomorrow.*"

Soo-ho nearly *collapsed.* "ARE YOU KIDDING ME?!"

Moonbin patted his back. "Welcome to Ji-ae's reign of terror, bro."

Ji-ae clapped her hands. "Alright, break time's over! Back to practice!"

Soo-ho sighed dramatically. "I should've *never* let you be my manager."

Ji-ae leaned in and whispered, "But then who else would make sure you become the best idol ever?"

Soo-ho blinked.

And just like that, he was reminded *why* he fell for her in the first place.

Even if she was an *absolute menace.*

Ji-ae's Secret Debut as JINNIE

The moment Ji-ae had been waiting for was finally here.

For weeks, she had been training in secret—vocals, choreography, stage presence—preparing for the biggest surprise of her life. And now, she was standing backstage at one of BLACKPINK's biggest concerts, dressed in a stunning black and silver outfit, her heart pounding against her chest.

She could hear the deafening cheers of fans as BLACKPINK performed their hit song. Ji-ae took a deep breath, feeling Jisoo's reassuring hand squeeze hers.

"You got this, Jinnie," Jisoo whispered with a wink. "He's going to lose his mind."

Ji-ae laughed nervously. "You think?"

"Oh, definitely." Lisa grinned. "He has no idea what's coming."

"Imagine his face when he realizes his *girlfriend* is the newest BLACKPINK member," Rosé giggled.

"I still can't believe you kept this a secret from him," Jennie smirked. "You're good."

Ji-ae smiled, a mix of excitement and nerves bubbling inside her. "Well, it's payback for him keeping ASTRO a secret from me."

Jisoo laughed. "Fair enough."

The music suddenly changed, and the stage lights dimmed. The audience grew confused as a special VCR played on the big screen.

A deep, familiar voice filled the arena.

"Introducing BLACKPINK's newest member... JINNIE!"

The crowd erupted into screams just as the lights flashed back on—and Ji-ae stepped onto the stage.

Dressed in the same edgy yet elegant style as the rest of BLACKPINK, Ji-ae held her mic close, her heart racing as the intro of their new song played. The girls turned to her with excited smiles, and with that, she sang her very first line as an official member of BLACKPINK.

And somewhere in the audience, completely stunned, was Soo-ho.

His jaw had *completely* dropped. His bandmates, ASTRO, were laughing and nudging him, but he couldn't react. He was too busy staring at his girlfriend, who was now standing on stage, *as part of BLACKPINK.*

"What the—" he started, but his voice was drowned by the cheers.

Ji-ae saw him.

And she winked.

Soo-ho's soul *left* his body.

"She—WHAT—WHEN—HOW?!" he spluttered, looking around in disbelief.

"She got you GOOD, bro!" Moonbin cackled.

Soo-ho ran a hand through his hair, watching as Ji-ae danced effortlessly with the girls, owning the stage like she was born to be there.

Then, just when he thought he had recovered, Ji-ae smirked directly at him before flawlessly hitting a high note.

Soo-ho groaned, sinking into his seat. "I'm never winning against her, am I?"

Sanha patted his shoulder. "Nope. And that's why you love her."

Soo-ho sighed dramatically but couldn't hide his proud smile.

Because, honestly?

Yeah.

He *really* did.

— ??? —

Chapter: The Songs That Bind Us ??

Callin' You (Tamally Maak) – JINNIE x Cha Eun-woo

Ji-ae sat in MOVE Entertainment's private studio, her fingers gently tapping on the microphone. She had been thinking about this for a while now—a song that spoke from her heart, one that reflected her journey, her emotions... and most importantly, her love for Soo-ho.

And who better to help bring it to life than him?

Soo-ho sat at the piano, adjusting his headphones. His fingers glided over the keys, playing the first few chords, a soft and soulful melody filling the room.

Ji-ae closed her eyes, letting the rhythm sink into her bones before she took a deep breath and began to sing.

? Tumse juda na main hoon sakti, haan...
(I can never be apart from you...)
? Har saans mein tu hai shaamil, jaaniya...
(You are in every breath I take, my love...)

Soo-ho glanced up at her, completely mesmerized. Her voice carried so much raw emotion, every note filled with love and longing.

As he continued playing, he started layering different instrumentals into the mix, adjusting the sound until it felt just *right*. He had never seen Ji-ae this passionate about a song before, and it made his heart race.

? Tumse hi roshan mera jahaan...
(You light up my entire world...)
? Tumse hi jeena mera asaan...
(With you, living feels easy...)

When she reached the chorus, Soo-ho—completely lost in the moment—hummed along with her, nodding to the beat. Ji-ae's eyes flickered open, and they met his gaze. A soft smile tugged at her lips.

As the song reached its final note, the studio fell silent except for the quiet hum of the recording equipment.

Ji-ae took off her headphones. "So... what do you think?"

Soo-ho stared at her for a long moment, then grinned. "You just created magic."

Ji-ae flushed, looking away. "You helped."

He leaned closer. "I don't think I've ever been more proud of you."

Her heart flipped.

This song... *their* song, was something special.

And deep inside, she knew—it was just the beginning.

Callin' You (Tamally Maak) – JINNIE & Cha Eun-woo Live Concert ???

The stadium was packed, fans holding up glowing pink and blue lightsticks, waving them in sync with the music playing softly in the background. The atmosphere buzzed with anticipation. Everyone knew something special was about to happen.

Soo-ho stood backstage, adjusting his in-ear monitor. He wasn't used to this—being on stage as *Cha Eun-woo*, standing in front of thousands of fans. He was used to composing, playing instruments, and singing in the background.

But tonight was different.

Tonight, he was performing with *her*.

Ji-ae—no, *JINNIE*—stood beside him, dressed in a breathtaking white and silver outfit that shimmered under the lights. She looked at him and smiled, gently squeezing his hand. "Ready?"

Soo-ho exhaled, calming his nerves. "Yeah. As long as you don't mess up."

Ji-ae gasped. "*Me*?! mess up?! Excuse me, *Cha Eun-woo*, but I'm the main vocalist here."

He chuckled. "Then let's give them something to remember."

The stage lights dimmed. The intro music started playing—soft piano, warm and nostalgic.

A single spotlight illuminated Ji-ae as she took center stage. She lifted the mic to her lips and, with closed eyes, began to sing.

? *Tumse juda na main hoon sakti, haan...*
(*I can never be apart from you...*)
? *Har saans mein tu hai shaamil, jaaniya...*
(*You are in every breath I take, my love...*)

The audience fell into a stunned silence, completely mesmerized.

Then, another spotlight turned on.

Soo-ho stepped forward, his voice smooth and deep as he harmonized with her.

? *Tumse hi roshan mera jahaan...*
(You light up my entire world...)
? *Tumse hi jeena mera asaan...*
(With you, living feels easy...)

The melody swelled, the music intensifying as the song reached its chorus. Ji-ae turned toward him, their eyes meeting as they sang together.

? *Main tera hoon, har pal...*
(I am yours, in every moment...)
? *Tu mera hai, hamesha...*
(You are mine, forever...)

Soo-ho smiled softly as he played the final notes on his guitar. Ji-ae took a deep breath, her voice carrying the last, lingering note.

The crowd erupted into cheers, chanting their names, holding up banners that read:

? **"JINNIE & CHA EUN-WOO – THE BEST DUO!"** ?

Ji-ae laughed breathlessly, turning to Soo-ho. "That was incredible."

Soo-ho smirked. "Told you I wouldn't mess up."

She rolled her eyes but couldn't hide her smile.

And then, in front of thousands of fans, without thinking, Ji-ae grabbed his hand and raised it high into the air.

The fans screamed even louder.

And somewhere deep in their hearts, they both knew—this moment, this song, and this feeling... it was forever.

Earthquake – JINNIE's Solo Concert

The stadium lights dimmed. The crowd erupted into cheers, the sound vibrating through the entire arena.

Soo-ho sat in the front row, his heart pounding in his chest. He adjusted his phone, pressing record as the stage lit up with a single spotlight.

And then... there she was.

JINNIE.

Ji-ae stood in the center of the stage, dressed in an all-black, sleek outfit that shimmered under the lights. She took a deep breath as the first notes of *Earthquake* filled the air.

And then she began.

? I feel your eyes on me, I feel the energy
? Body on gravity, right where it's meant to be

Her voice was powerful, filled with confidence and passion. The crowd chanted along, completely immersed in her performance.

Soo-ho, still recording, mouthed the lyrics with her. His gaze never left her—not even for a second.

? My heart beats like an earthquake
? Every time you're near, I just can't escape
? You shake me up, make me break
? Boy, you're my earthquake...

Ji-ae's eyes scanned the crowd, and when she spotted *him,* her lips curled into a smirk. Soo-ho grinned back, still singing along.

As the chorus hit, Ji-ae's confidence soared. The backup dancers moved in sync, the stage lights flashing to the beat.

Soo-ho knew this wasn't just a song—this was her dream coming true.

And he was going to support her *every step of the way.*

The final note rang through the stadium, and Ji-ae stood there, breathless, as the audience erupted into applause.

Soo-ho put down his phone and cupped his hands around his mouth.

"JINNIE JJANG!!"

Ji-ae laughed, shaking her head before blowing a kiss in his direction.

Yeah.

This was only the beginning of something legendary.

ASTRO's Concert – Starring Cha Eun-woo ??

The crowd **exploded** with cheers as the lights dimmed, the anticipation in the air electric. Fans waved their glowing purple lightsticks, chanting **"ASTRO! ASTRO! ASTRO!"** in perfect sync. The stage lit up with a burst of fireworks, and then—

The band appeared.

Soo-ho—*Cha Eun-woo*—stood front and center, dressed in an all-black outfit with silver chains, his jawline looking sharper than ever under the neon lights. The moment he grabbed the mic, the entire stadium *screamed*.

But as he scanned the audience, his **eyes landed on her.**

Ji-ae—**his Ji-ae.**

She sat in the front row, glowing under the golden lights. Her dress was *breathtaking*—a sleek, sparkling silver gown that hugged her figure perfectly. Her hair cascaded down in soft waves, and her lips curled into that **mischievous** smirk he knew too well.

And oh, she **knew** exactly what she was doing to him.

She was **recording him**, phone in hand, **lip-syncing** every word he was about to sing, mouthing the lyrics like it was **her** song.

And just like that...

Soo-ho completely **forgot** what he was supposed to do.

"Eun-woo, let's go!" One of his bandmates nudged him, snapping him back to reality. The music had started, the intro playing, and he was supposed to sing.

Soo-ho cursed under his breath. Ji-ae **laughed.**

Oh, she was enjoying this way too much.

Finally, he pulled himself together, gripping the mic tighter as he started the first verse.

? Baby, can't you see the way you're making me lose my mind?
? Every time I look at you, I lose track of time...

His eyes never left her.

Ji-ae grinned, still recording him, still **lip-syncing** along, mouthing the words as if she were the one performing.

And when the chorus hit, Soo-ho **pointed straight at her.**

? You're the earthquake shaking up my world...
? No matter where you are, you're still my girl...

The fans **went wild.**

Ji-ae's eyes widened slightly, and for the first time that night, **her face turned red.**

But Soo-ho wasn't done.

He moved **closer** to the edge of the stage, still singing, but his focus was **only on her.** Ji-ae, realizing she was about to **die of embarrassment**, held up her phone in front of her face to hide.

Too bad Soo-ho **reached down and pulled it away.**

The crowd *screamed.* Ji-ae gasped.

And then, with a smirk, **he winked at her.**

Ji-ae **officially malfunctioned.**

Soo-ho collapsed onto the couch in the dressing room, running a hand through his damp hair. His heartbeat was still racing—not just from the concert, but from **her.**

Ji-ae.

She walked in with that same mischievous glint in her eyes, holding up her phone. "So... explain why you looked like a lovesick puppy the entire time?"

Soo-ho groaned, covering his face. "You're never letting me live this down, are you?"

Ji-ae plopped down beside him, grinning. "Nope. Not when you literally pointed at me during the chorus and made the whole stadium scream. I was NOT prepared for that."

Soo-ho peeked at her through his fingers. "You think *you* weren't prepared? Do you have any idea how hard it was to focus when you were sitting there looking like that?" He motioned to her dress, his ears turning slightly pink.

Ji-ae giggled, leaning her head on his shoulder. "Well, you still did amazing."

Soo-ho turned his head to look at her. "You really think so?"

Ji-ae smiled softly. "I know so. I'm really proud of you, Soo-ho."

His heart melted.

Without thinking, he reached up and gently tucked a loose strand of her hair behind her ear. His fingers lingered for a second before he sighed dramatically. "Still... you *did* almost ruin my concert."

Ji-ae gasped. "Me?! YOU were the one getting distracted!"

He smirked. "Because you were being *unfair*."

Ji-ae rolled her eyes. "Oh please, how was I unfair?"

Soo-ho turned to fully face her, his gaze soft. "You were sitting there looking way too beautiful, singing along to my lyrics, recording me with that smile of yours… what was I supposed to do?"

Ji-ae's breath hitched. Her cheeks warmed.

And then, without thinking, he reached out and poked her cheek. "You're crazy."

Ji-ae blinked, surprised, then suddenly grabbed his hand, intertwining their fingers. "Yeah, but I'm your crazy."

Soo-ho's heart exploded.

She squeezed his hand, resting her head back on his shoulder.

They sat there in comfortable silence, the sound of distant fans still echoing outside the stadium.

Soo-ho suddenly chuckled. "So… are we calling this even, or do I still owe you for distracting me?"

Ji-ae grinned. "Oh, you definitely still owe me."

Soo-ho smirked. "Fine. Name your price."

Ji-ae thought for a moment before her eyes twinkled. "Ice cream. Lots of it."

Soo-ho laughed, pressing a quick kiss to the top of her head. "Deal."

And just like that, they stayed there—hand in hand, hearts full, and completely lost in their own world.

BLACKPINK's First Concert with JINNIE!

The energy in the stadium was electric. Fans waved their lightsticks, chanting "BLACKPINK! BLACKPINK!" at the top of their lungs. The massive LED screens flashed images of the four legendary members—Jisoo, Jennie, Rosé, Lisa—and now, their newest addition: JINNIE.

Ji-ae took a deep breath, gripping her mic. This was it—her first full concert as a BLACKPINK member.

Jisoo squeezed her hand. "You ready?"

Ji-ae exhaled, nodding. "Let's kill it."

The stage lit up as the beat dropped. The girls stepped forward, owning the spotlight. Ji-ae's heart pounded with excitement as they performed hit after hit—Shut Down, DDU-DU DDU-DU, Tally, Pink Venom—the crowd screamed their lyrics.

Then came her solo stage.

The intro of Earthquake blasted through the speakers, and the stadium roared. Ji-ae stood under the spotlight, her silhouette shimmering in a stunning black and silver outfit. The moment she started singing, the entire audience went wild.

But there was one person missing.

Soo-ho.

She searched the crowd while singing, expecting to see him in the front row like always. But he wasn't there.

Where was he?

The song ended with a powerful high note, and she struck her final pose, chest heaving. The audience erupted in cheers and applause.

And then—

A voice came from the back of the arena.

"KANG JI-AE!"

Her eyes widened. That voice...

The crowd parted slightly, and standing among them, disguised in a hoodie and cap, was Soo-ho. He grinned, pulling down his mask and revealing his ridiculously handsome face.

Ji-ae's heart stopped.

The audience gasped, realizing who he was. The screens zoomed in on him, and the entire stadium exploded with screams.

Soo-ho cupped his hands around his mouth. "JINNIE, YOU KILLED IT!"

Ji-ae's hands flew to her face, a rush of shock, happiness, and disbelief crashing over her. She hadn't expected him to come at all—and now here he was, surprising her in the best way possible.

Lisa laughed, nudging her. "Go to him, duh!"

Ji-ae didn't hesitate. She ran down the stage steps, straight towards him.

Soo-ho caught her as she threw herself into his arms, hugging him tight. The audience screamed louder, their cheers turning into happy chaos.

"You idiot!" she whispered against his shoulder, tearing up. "Why didn't you tell me?!"

He smirked, pulling back slightly to look at her. "Because surprising you is way more fun."

Ji-ae punched his arm lightly, her heart bursting with emotions. "You're the worst."

Soo-ho grinned, wiping a tear off her cheek. "And yet, you're still in my arms."

Ji-ae rolled her eyes but smiled. "Shut up and just hold me."

Soo-ho pulled her closer, ignoring the thousands of fans watching. "Always."

BLACKPINK CONCERT CHAOS: WHEN JINNIE AND CHA EUN-WOO BROKE THE INTERNET!

Ji-ae clung to Soo-ho, her heart racing. The moment felt **too perfect**, too unreal. The lights, the screams, the **pure euphoria** of the concert—everything had led up to this.

And then—

Soo-ho **tilted her chin up**, his eyes **burning** with something deep, something unspoken.

"Ji-ae," he whispered.

Her breath hitched. "Yeah?"

His gaze flickered to her lips, then back to her eyes, as if **asking for permission.**

Ji-ae **didn't hesitate.**

She grabbed the collar of his hoodie and **pulled him down—**

And **kissed him.**

The stadium **erupted.**

Screams. Cheers. Absolute chaos.

Some fans were **crying**, some were **freaking out**, and others were just **SHOOK to their core.** Phones were **whipping out** from every direction, capturing the **most**

insane moment in BLACKPINK concert history.

Jisoo, Jennie, Lisa, and Rosé stood on stage, **watching with jaws on the floor.**

Jisoo: *"Did she—did they just—?"*
Jennie: *"OH MY GOD??"*
Lisa: *"SOMEONE SCREEN RECORD THIS RIGHT NOW."*
Rosé: *"This is going viral in exactly three seconds."*

Meanwhile, the audience was in **full-blown meltdown mode**:

- *"I CAN'T BREATHE. I CAN'T BREATHE."*
- *"JINNIE AND CHA EUN-WOO ARE REAL OMGGGGG."*
- *"SOMEONE CHECK ON THE INTERNET IT JUST CRASHED."*
- *"DO YOU HEAR ME SCREAMING THROUGH THE SCREEN???"*

When Ji-ae **finally pulled away**, Soo-ho was **grinning like an idiot.**

"Wow," he breathed. "I should surprise you more often."

Ji-ae **laughed breathlessly**, still feeling the rush of the moment.

Then—

Lisa's voice boomed through the mic: **"OKAY, Y'ALL JUST WITNESSED HISTORY."**

The crowd **lost their minds all over again.**

Ji-ae **hid her face in Soo-ho's chest**, giggling as he wrapped his arms around her, holding her **like she was the most precious thing in the world.**

And just like that, their **legendary** love story became **the most iconic moment in K-pop history.**

Chapter: The Unexpected News

Ji-ae stretched her arms as she sat in the cozy living room, curled up on the couch. BLACKPINK had just finished a world tour, and ASTRO was wrapping up their promotions, which meant she and Soo-ho finally had time to themselves.

But something felt... off.

Her stomach churned slightly, and for the past few days, she had been feeling strangely exhausted. Even Jisoo had raised an eyebrow when Ji-ae passed out on the couch mid-conversation.

Then, there was the thing with food.

"Ugh, I swear this ramen tastes like socks," Ji-ae groaned, pushing her plate away.

Lisa gasped dramatically. "EXCUSE ME?! You *love* ramen!"

Rosé narrowed her eyes. "Wait... tired all the time, weird cravings, hating your favorite food..."

Jennie's eyes widened. "Ji-ae... when was your last—"

Ji-ae nearly choked. "*NO WAY!*"

The girls exchanged looks before Jisoo calmly placed a pregnancy test in front of her.

"Test. Now."

Ji-ae blinked. "Why do you just... have one?"

Jisoo shrugged. "You never know when things get *interesting.*"

And so, with a deep breath, Ji-ae grabbed the test and went to the bathroom.

Five minutes later.

She stared at the two pink lines, her heart pounding in her chest.

"Oh my God," she whispered.

She was pregnant.

Chapter: The 'Telling Soo-ho' Disaster

Telling Soo-ho was going to be *fine.*

At least... that's what she thought.

The plan was simple: she'd cook a nice dinner, set the mood, and break the news gently. Maybe even film his reaction because it would be *hilarious.*

But, as expected, things **did *not*** go as planned.

Soo-ho entered their apartment, exhausted from a long day at practice, throwing his bag on the couch. "Jagiya, I swear, Moonbin almost dropped me during the last move—"

"*I'M PREGNANT!*" Ji-ae blurted out.

Silence.

Soo-ho froze mid-step, blinking like his brain had short-circuited. "You're... you're what?"

"I *said* I'm pregnant!"

Another long pause. Then:

Soo-ho let out a loud *THUD* as he collapsed onto the couch, looking like he had been hit by a truck. His mouth opened and closed like a fish gasping for air.

Ji-ae bit her lip. "Uh... say something?"

Soo-ho took a deep breath, then—

"AAAAAAAAAAAAAAAAAAAAAAAAAAAAAAAAAAAAAAAAAA!!!!"

Ji-ae winced. "Can you *not* scream like we're in a horror movie?"

Soo-ho jumped up, grabbing her shoulders. "YOU'RE HAVING A BABY?!"

She nodded.

"LIKE—A *REAL* BABY? *OUR* BABY?!"

She nodded again.

And just like that, Soo-ho dramatically *fainted.*

Ji-ae groaned. "Oh, for the love of—"

Just then, the apartment door burst open, revealing Jisoo, Lisa, Jennie, and Rosé, who had apparently been *spying* the whole time.

Lisa clapped her hands. "*Called it.*"

As expected, telling their friends and family was a complete mess.

Denise screamed so loudly that *Madeline nearly punched her out of panic.*

JianHao choked on his drink, and Debbie had to perform the Heimlich maneuver on him.

Su-jin and Su-ah just *stood there,* jaws dropped, before they started aggressively planning baby outfits.

Soo-ho, meanwhile, had entered full *overprotective dad mode.*

"You're *not* lifting anything heavier than a spoon."

"Soo-ho, it's just my phone."

"Nope. Too heavy."

At one point, he tried to *forbid* Ji-ae from even walking.

"Soo-ho, if you don't let go of me, I will personally strangle you."

"But—but *what if you trip?*"

Ji-ae groaned. "I TRIP EVERY DAY. THIS IS NOTHING NEW."

It didn't help that their friends encouraged the chaos.

Jisoo whispered to Soo-ho, "You know, pregnant women have the weirdest cravings. Maybe she'll want—"

"I'M ON IT!" Soo-ho ran out the door before Ji-ae could even say what she wanted.

Jennie smirked. "Too easy."

Fast forward **nine months later.**

It was **absolute mayhem.**

Ji-ae's contractions started in the *middle* of BLACKPINK's rehearsal, and everyone *lost their minds.*

Lisa: "OH MY GOD, IT'S HAPPENING."

Jisoo: *"SOMEONE CALL SOO-HO, STAT!"*

Jennie: *"WHERE ARE HER BAGS? WHERE ARE HER BAGS?!"*

Rosé: *crying in the corner* "She's growing up so fast..."

Meanwhile, Soo-ho was at an ASTRO fan meeting when he got the call.

Manager: "You can't just leave mid-event, Soo-ho—"

Soo-ho: **"MY WIFE IS IN LABOR, MOVE OUT OF MY WAY!!!"**

He *sprinted* out of the venue, leaving fans screaming in confusion.

By the time he reached the hospital, Ji-ae was already in full *rage mode.*

"Soo-ho," she growled.

"Yes, jagiya (babe/darling)?" he asked sweetly.

"I SWEAR, IF YOU DON'T GET THIS BABY OUT OF ME *RIGHT NOW,* I WILL PERSONALLY END YOU."

Soo-ho paled. "D-Doctor?! We need help here!!!"

Chapter: Meeting Anaya Ji-eun Lee

Hours later, after enough screaming to *terrify an entire city,* a soft cry finally filled the room.

Soo-ho's breath hitched as the doctor gently placed their daughter in Ji-ae's arms.

She was **perfect.**

Tiny. Beautiful. With the softest little hands and Soo-ho's ridiculously pretty eyes.

Ji-ae, exhausted but smiling, whispered, "Hi, baby girl…"

Soo-ho, completely overwhelmed, wiped away a tear. "She's so… *tiny.*"

Jisoo, Lisa, Jennie, and Rosé peeked in through the window, all *ugly crying.*

Denise, Debbie, and Madeline were dramatically fanning themselves.

JianHao, meanwhile, had fainted for some reason.

Soo-ho leaned down, pressing a soft kiss to Ji-ae's forehead. "You did amazing."

Ji-ae smirked weakly. "Yeah, yeah... you *owe* me for this, though."

Soo-ho grinned. "Anything for my girls."

And just like that, their little family officially began. ?

Diwali Night – Anaya's First Word ??

The Lee household was glowing with golden lights, diyas lined up across every surface, and the scent of sweets filling the air. Ji-ae, dressed in a gorgeous red and gold saree, held little Anaya in her arms, bouncing her gently. Soo-ho stood beside her, wearing a black sherwani, watching the fireworks light up the night sky.

Their friends had gathered to celebrate, all dressed in traditional Indian outfits. Denise and Debbie were busy taking selfies, JianHao was sneaking extra gulab jamuns, and Su-jin and Su-ah were helping set up sparklers.

"Alright, Anaya, are you ready to see the fireworks?" Ji-ae cooed, adjusting the tiny lehenga Anaya was wearing.

Anaya, barely a year old, blinked up at the sky, her big brown eyes reflecting the colorful lights bursting above. She kicked her little feet excitedly, her chubby hands reaching out.

Soo-ho chuckled. "She looks mesmerized."

Just then, a massive firework shot up, exploding into a cascade of shimmering gold and silver. The entire crowd gasped in awe.

And then—

"Lights!"

Silence.

Ji-ae and Soo-ho froze.

Everyone turned to look at Anaya, who was still staring at the sky with wide eyes, clapping her hands together.

Ji-ae's heart skipped a beat. "Did she just—"

"Did she say 'lights'?" Soo-ho gasped, his jaw dropping.

Anaya giggled and repeated, "Lights! Lights!" pointing at the fireworks.

Everyone burst into cheers. JianHao started clapping. "Ayo, first word! Let's gooo!"

Denise squealed. "That's the cutest thing EVER!"

Debbie was already recording the whole thing on her phone. "Ji-ae, Soo-ho, how does it feel to have the most adorable baby on the planet?"

Ji-ae, overwhelmed with happiness, turned to Soo-ho, tears brimming in her eyes. "That was her first word…"

Soo-ho, looking just as emotional, scooped Anaya into his arms and spun her around. "That's my girl! You said your first word, and it was 'lights'! Just like your mama."

Ji-ae laughed, wiping her tears. "It really runs in the family, huh?"

Anaya, still excited, kept pointing at the fireworks, chanting, "Lights! Lights!"

Ji-ae leaned into Soo-ho's side, wrapping her arms around him. "This is the best Diwali ever."

Soo-ho kissed her forehead. "And just the beginning of many more."

As more fireworks filled the sky, Anaya kept repeating her new favorite word, while their friends cheered and celebrated, capturing the unforgettable moment.

Ji-ae and Soo-ho couldn't stop smiling.

Their little family was perfect. ?

It was late at night, the soft glow of a nightlight illuminating the cozy music studio in their home. Ji-ae sat on the couch, gently rocking Anaya in her arms, humming a soothing melody while Soo-ho strummed his guitar beside her.

"She always calms down when you sing," Soo-ho whispered, watching as Anaya's tiny fingers curled around Ji-ae's necklace.

Ji-ae smiled. "Music runs in her blood. Just like us."

Soo-ho chuckled, setting his guitar down for a moment. "You know... we should write a song for her."

Ji-ae's eyes lit up. "A song? About Anaya?"

"Yeah," Soo-ho said, his voice soft. "Something just for her. Something she can listen to when she grows up and know how much we love her."

Ji-ae's heart melted. "That's the sweetest thing you've ever said."

Soo-ho smirked. "I have my moments."

Ji-ae playfully rolled her eyes before looking down at their baby girl, who was peacefully dozing off in her arms. "Alright. Let's do it."

Soo-ho picked up his guitar again, his fingers lightly plucking the strings as he found a gentle melody. Ji-ae closed her eyes, listening to the tune, letting the emotions guide her. And then, she began to sing softly:

**"Little star in my sky, shining oh so bright,
With every smile, you light up my life tonight.
Tiny hands, tiny feet, but a heart so wide,
You're my forever, my love, my lullaby."**

Soo-ho looked at her in awe. "That was perfect."

Ji-ae blushed. "I just sang what I feel."

Soo-ho grinned and started adding harmonies, tweaking the chords to match the softness of her voice. He sang the next part:

**"I'll be your shelter when the rain falls down,
I'll be your laughter when there's no one around.
No matter where you go, no matter how far,
You'll always be my shining star."**

Ji-ae wiped a tear from her eye. "Soo-ho, that's beautiful."

Soo-ho reached over and tucked a strand of hair behind her ear. "It's how I feel. She's our little star."

Ji-ae looked down at Anaya, who was sleeping peacefully, completely unaware of the song her parents were creating just for her.

Soo-ho chuckled. "I think she likes it."

Ji-ae laughed softly. "Maybe one day, she'll sing it back to us."

Soo-ho leaned over and pressed a gentle kiss to Ji-ae's forehead. "Then let's make it the best song ever."

And so, that night, in the quiet warmth of their home, Ji-ae and Soo-ho poured their hearts into a melody that would forever be theirs—an everlasting lullaby for their little girl. ??

ChatGPT said:

BLACKPINK vs. ASTRO – The Ultimate Battle for Anaya's Favorite! ???

Ji-ae and Soo-ho should have *seen it coming*. With Anaya growing up surrounded by both BLACKPINK and ASTRO, it was only a matter of time before the ultimate showdown began—**who was her favorite?!**

It all started one evening at their home, where the BLACKPINK girls and ASTRO members had gathered for a casual get-together. Everything was going *fine*—until Eun-woo (Soo-ho) *accidentally* asked:

"Anaya, who's your favorite—ASTRO or BLACKPINK?"

The room went *dead silent*. Then chaos.

"YA! WHY WOULD YOU ASK HER THAT?!" Ji-ae gasped, smacking his arm.

Jisoo dramatically placed a hand over her heart. "As her **favorite aunt**, I already *know* it's BLACKPINK."

Lisa crossed her arms smugly. "Pfft. Of course. She's literally **JINNIE's** daughter. She was BORN to be a Blink."

"HEY, HOLD ON!" MJ of ASTRO pointed at them. "JINNIE wouldn't even *exist* if Soo-ho wasn't in ASTRO first! That makes **us** her rightful favorites!"

"She literally danced to *Ddu-du Ddu-du* first," Jennie argued, smirking. "Case closed."

"But she fell asleep to ASTRO's songs *every night* when she was a baby," JinJin countered.

At this point, Anaya, the *unintentional cause* of this war, sat happily in Ji-ae's lap, completely **oblivious** to the battle raging around her.

Soo-ho smirked and leaned in toward Ji-ae. "Should we stop them?"

Ji-ae glanced at the absolute **mess** happening in their living room—Lisa and Cha Eun-woo *arguing over choreography*, Jisoo and Moonbin *trying to bribe Anaya with toys*, and Rosé singing a BLACKPINK song *while* Rocky beatboxed an ASTRO track to see which one made Anaya dance first.

She shook her head. "Nope. This is way too entertaining."

Finally, **the decision had to be made**.

Jisoo clapped her hands. "Okay, okay, everyone *calm down*! We'll settle this the only way that makes sense."

Everyone leaned in, waiting for the verdict.

Ji-ae turned to Anaya. "Baby, say the name of your favorite."

Anaya blinked at them, looked at her mom, then her dad, then at all her **crazy** aunts and uncles.

Then, she smiled and said,

"Bella."

...Her beagle. ?

The room *exploded* with laughter.

Ji-ae wiped away tears. "Well, there you have it. **Bella wins.**"

Soo-ho nodded solemnly. "The true queen of this household."

BLACKPINK and ASTRO groaned in defeat. But instead of giving up, they turned to **Bella**, now napping peacefully on the couch.

Jisoo smirked. "Okay, new plan. **We make Bella choose.**"

And just like that, the **battle continued.** ?

The Everlasting Love Story of Ji-ae & Soo-ho ??

Through every storm, every high and low, and every ridiculous argument over who Anaya loved more, Ji-ae and Soo-ho's journey had been nothing short of a *beautiful* mess—a story filled with drama, laughter, and an endless amount of love.

From their school days at Titan Academy, where they first bickered and blushed, to their *unexpected* rise in the entertainment industry, they had been through it all. **Confessions under the stars. Secret gigs. Late-night songwriting sessions. A surprise BLACKPINK debut. Chaotic concerts where one kept distracting the other.**

And then came Anaya—their little miracle, the light of their lives, the one who *somehow* managed to turn BLACKPINK and ASTRO into full-time babysitters.

Life was anything but *calm* with them. Ji-ae still had her fiery attitude, and Soo-ho was still an absolute *simp* for her. But their love? **Unshakable.**

As the years passed, they watched Anaya grow, their careers thrive, and their love story continue—because this wasn't just a romance. **It was a forever kind of love.**

No matter what the world threw at them, Ji-ae and Soo-ho had each other. And as they stood together, watching the fireworks light up the sky on another Diwali night, with Anaya giggling in their arms, they knew—

This was their happily ever after. ???

Contents

www.ingramcontent.com/pod-product-compliance
Lightning Source LLC
Chambersburg PA
CBHW031148160726
47991CB00004B/1587